Ohio

OHIO BY ROAD

NATIONAL FOREST

0 10 20 30 40 50 60 70
MILES

Celebrate the States

Ohio

Victoria Sherrow

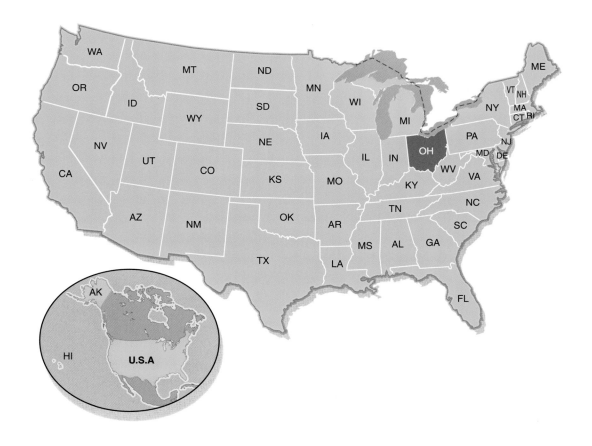

mc Marshall Cavendish
Benchmark
New York

Marshall Cavendish Benchmark
99 White Plains Road
Tarrytown, NY 10591-9001
www.marshallcavendish.us

All Internet addresses were correct and accurate at the time of printing.

Library of Congress Cataloging-in-Publication Data
Sherrow, Victoria.
Ohio / by Victoria Sherrow.—2nd ed.
p. cm.—(Celebrate the states)
"Provides comprehensive information on the geography, history, wildlife, governmental structure, economy, cultural diversity, peoples, religion, and landmarks of Ohio"—Provided by publisher.
Includes bibliographical references and index.
Audience: Grades 7-8
ISBN-13: 978-0-7614-2558-8
1. Ohio—Juvenile literature. I. Title. II. Series.
F491.3.S472007
977.1—dc22   2006034103

Editor: Christine Florie
Publisher: Michelle Bisson
Art Director: Anahid Hamparian
Series Designer: Adam Mietlowski

Photo research by Connie Gardner

Cover Photo: Danita Delimont Stock Photography/IAN ADAMS

The photographs in this book are used by permission and courtesy of: *SuperStock:* Richard Cummins, back cover; age footstock, 99, 111(B); Prisma, 114, 119. *Alamy:* Danita Delimont, 8; James Frank, 11; Dennis MacDonald, 17, 89, 97; Tom Till, 20; NorthWind Picture Archive, 35; Jeff Greenberg, 52, 67, 121; Tom Tracy Photography, 86; David Frazier, 107. *Getty Images:* Arthur Tress/Phototonica, 12; Hulton Archive, 44, 128; Eileen Kovchok, 55; Courtney Boucher, 68; Greg Pease/Stone, 82; Andy Saks/Stone, 85; Marc Romanelli, 92; Mike Powell, 126; Tim Klein, 130. *The Granger Collection:* 13, 26, 29, 31, 32, 36, 76. *AP Photo:* The Plain Dealer, Joshua Gunter, 16; Mike Elicson, 56; Kiichiro Sato, 80; Sidney Daily News, Erin Pence, 91; Eric Albrecht, 122. *Photo Researchers:* Scott Camazine, 19; A.H. Rider, 21. *PhotoEdit:* Jeff Greenberg, 50, 57. *Dembinsky Photo Associates:* Dominique Braud, 23; Jim Roetzel, 111(T); Bill Leaman, 115. *The Image Works:* Topham, 59; Andre Jenny, 65, 105; Jeff Greenberg, 94, 103, 109, 133. *NorthWind Picture Archive:* 30, 39, 42. *Corbis:* Poodles Rock, 38; Bettmann, 47, 48; Dieterien, 70; Lee Snider, 72; Dale Omori, 77; Kelly-Mooney Photography, 96; Ron Kuntz/Reuters, 101; Layne Kennedy, 102, 104; Ulrich Perrey/dpa, 123; Hulton Deutsch Collection, 125; David Muench, 136.

Printed in Malaysia
1 3 5 6 4 2

Contents

Ohio Is . . .

Ohio is a place where rolling plains, major rivers, and ports along Lake Erie have boosted agriculture and industry.

"The soil is extremely fertile and there is no region more happily situated for commercial enterprises."

—French traveler Alexis de Tocqueville, 1831

"Cleveland . . . is an important and flourishing city. Commercial advantages are great, the harbor excellent."

—artist John Kilburn, 1856

Ohio is the birthplace of many authors and artists . . .

"[My readers] are all aware of where I was born and brought up and they know that half of my books could not have been written if it had not been for the city of my birth."

—author and Columbus native James Thurber

"[Ohio] has been a matrix for me. Ohio also offers an escape from stereotyped black settings. It is neither plantation nor ghetto."

—author and Nobel laureate Toni Morrison

. . . and famous inventors.

"If I were giving a young man advice in how he might succeed in life, I would say to him, pick out a good father and mother, and begin life in Ohio."

—aviation pioneer Wilbur Wright, 1910

This sports-loving state gave birth to the National Football League and the nation's first professional baseball team . . .

"I'd rather be president of the Cincinnati Baseball Club than president of the United States."
                    —Cincinnati Red Stockings organizer Aaron B. Champion, 1868

. . . while its diverse musical heritage can be seen at the Rock and Roll Hall of Fame and the National Cleveland-Style Polka Hall of Fame.

"To much of the world, music in Cleveland means the Cleveland Orchestra, polka bands and rock and roll. But, over the years, Greater Cleveland has also made significant contributions to jazz—and continues to do so."
                    —jazz historian Joe Mosbrook, 1996

It is a state rich in people from many ethnic and religious groups—a melting pot like the nation itself.

"Ohio is a microcosm of the whole country—it's so diverse. That's why it's hard to get a handle on it."
                    —Congressman Ted Strickland (D-OH), 2006

Ohio has been blessed with natural resources and resourceful people. It is regarded as a down-to-earth place in the Midwest.

Around the state, cities house business and industry, along with centers for research, health care, the arts, and transportation. Small towns cherish their own traditions, and parts of southern Ohio reflect people's Appalachian roots. In Amish communities people still work their farms with horse-drawn plows. Columbus is now home to thousands of immigrants from Somalia. These places are all "Ohio."

Chapter One

Land of Plenty

The Reverend Manasseh Cutler first saw the land between Lake Erie and the Ohio River in the 1780s when it was part of the American frontier. Cutler, a director of the Ohio Company of Associates, declared that this land could be "the garden of the world, the seat of wealth, and the centre of a great Empire." In fact, the word *Ohio* comes from an Iroquois word that means "great river." Ohio would go on to play a key role in the life of a growing nation.

Once the gateway to the West, Ohio now forms the eastern part of the Midwest. The state is bordered on the north by Michigan and Lake Erie. To the south are West Virginia and Kentucky. Indiana lies to the west and Pennsylvania to the east. Throughout its history Ohio has benefited from waterways that connect it to other regions and from a wealth of raw materials.

ROLLING HILLS AND WOODS

Millions of years ago water covered Ohio. It eventually drained off, leaving behind swamps. Then came the Ice Age, when glaciers up to 8,000 feet thick covered two-thirds of Ohio.

The fertile soil of Ohio has given rise to acres of rich farmland.

Mammoths and mastodons, tall animals resembling elephants, roamed the land. Using their conelike teeth, they chewed on spruce trees that grew on ice-free patches of land. Scientists have found the bones of more than 150 mastodons in Ohio, some dating back more than 11,000 years.

When the last glacier receded from the area between 12,000 and 15,000 years ago, Ohio was left with several distinct regions. The Black Swamp, a wetland in the northwest just south of Toledo, is made up of swamps and marshes. The Till Plains region in the west contains some of the most fertile land in the country and is part of America's Corn Belt. The south is dotted by rivers and rugged hills, which attract many hikers. The north has both flat areas and gently rolling land, with productive soil that is good for growing fruits and vegetables. The flat Lake Plain lies in the northwest and along Lake Erie. Both were formed after glaciers left behind sand and soil near what was once a much larger lake.

Eastern Ohio is blessed with abundant mineral deposits, such as clay, coal, salt, and oil. During the late 1800s about half of the oil used throughout the nation came from Ohio. Along with coal and oil, natural gas provides another source of energy. Most of the state's natural gas has been produced in southeastern Ohio. Deposits of rock, mostly sandstone and limestone, have been used for buildings. Sand and crushed rocks have been available for making roads and concrete.

The first European settlers to arrive in Ohio found the region covered with lush forests, mostly of hardwood trees, such as beech, elm, ash, cherry, maple, hickory, and oak. Novelist Conrad Richter wrote that those early pioneers saw "a sea of solid treetops. . . . As far as the eye could reach, this lonely forest sea rolled on and on." Today, about one-fourth of the state remains wooded.

Northern Ohio farmers take advantage of the rich soil in this part of the state.

The horse chestnut tree, called the buckeye tree, gave Ohio its nickname, the Buckeye State. This tree's yellowish white flowers bloom in late spring and early summer. These blossoms then turn into nut-like seeds that are not safe to eat. The shiny, dark brown seed is said to resemble the eye of a deer or buck, which led to the name "buckeye." Early settlers found that buckeye wood was not suitable for building homes, but it was easy to carve. People used this wood to make cradles, chairs, and other pieces of furniture.

The nut-like seeds of the horse chestnut tree look very much like the eye of a deer, giving Ohio its nickname, the Buckeye State.

"A LABOR OF LOVE"

In 1806 the legendary John Chapman, known as Johnny Appleseed, came through Ohio during his famous walk across the frontier. With sacks full of apple seeds, he made his way down the Ohio River to the Muskingum River and across the state toward Indiana. Wherever he went he planted seeds so that future settlers could enjoy the flowers and fruit that had pleased him so much at his Pennsylvania home.

When Chapman died in 1845, Texas congressman Sam Houston made a speech about Johnny Appleseed's "labor of love" in the U.S. House of Representatives. He said, "This old man was one of the most useful citizens of the world in his humble way." Because of Johnny Appleseed, hundreds of thousands of acres of apple trees now grow in Ohio. Their fragrant pink and white blossoms fill orchards every spring.

Fir trees also abound in the state, including Douglas fir trees and various kinds of pine and spruce trees. A popular story out of Wooster holds that the American tradition of the Christmas tree began there in 1847. August Imgard, a German immigrant, cut down a spruce tree and adorned it with candles, delighting his neighbors. The idea spread throughout Ohio and other parts of the country. Today, people can visit tree farms to select a tree for the holiday season.

Ohioans in rural or wooded areas see plenty of wild creatures, including white-tailed deer, rabbit, fox, coyote, raccoon, opossum, and beaver. Chipmunks and squirrels dart across lawns during the warm months. The endangered bald eagle lives in Ohio, as does the bobcat. Bird-watchers can spot cardinals, woodpeckers, larks, hawks, and owls.

ABUNDANT WATERS

Ohio is blessed with abundant rivers and streams. In the north the Maumee, Sandusky, Vermilion, and Cuyahoga rivers flow into Lake Erie. Most waters in the south, including the Great Miami, Scioto, Hocking, and Muskingum rivers, drain into the Ohio.

Lake Erie is the best-known lake in Ohio. Besides providing transportation, the lake yields tons of fish. One fish is so plentiful that Lake Erie has been called the Walleye Capital of the World. Most of Ohio's other lakes are small, but the state has many larger man-made lakes, chiefly in the east. Grand Lake Saint Marys is the largest artificial body of water in the world built without machinery. It was created between 1830 and 1845 by damming several rivers. About 1,700 workers, mostly Irish and German immigrants, used pickaxes and shovels to move vast amounts of earth. Oxen and horses carried the earth to where the dams were being formed. The lake is 9 miles long and nearly 3 miles wide.

LAND AND WATER

Ashtabula

Lake Erie

Toledo

Lorain · Cleveland
Sandusky · Parma
Bowling Green
Pymatuning Reservoir
Shenango River Lake
Warren
Maumee R.
Akron
Findlay
Youngstown
Auglaize R.
Berlin Lake
Alliance
Massillon · Canton
Lima
Mansfield
Charles Mill Lake
East Liverpool
Sandusky R.
Marion
Indian Lake
Scioto R.
Killbuck R.
Sugar R.
Grand Lake St. Marys
Steubenville
Alum Creek L.
Tuscarawas R.
Ohio R.
Great Miami R.
Newark
Dillon Lake
Cambridge
Springfield
Licking R.
Zanesville
Buckeye Lake
Columbus
Dayton
Lancaster
Muskingum R.
Middletown
Marietta
Chillicothe
Athens
Cincinnati
Point R.
Rocky Fork Lake
Scioto R.
Ohio R.
Ohio R.
Portsmouth

| 0 – 500 ft. | | | | | | | |

0 10 20 30 40 50 60 70
MILES

In this water-rich state it's no surprise that many Ohioans enjoy fishing. Besides walleye, they can go after bass, pike, trout, perch, catfish, sunfish, bluegill, and crappie. "I believe I've caught just about every type of fish we have in Ohio by now," said one seventy-six-year-old fisherman. People also use the state's lakes and rivers for swimming, sailing, boating, canoeing, and waterskiing.

"People know our lakes and rivers, but many have never heard of our beautiful waterfalls," said Columbus native Jack Wheeler. These falls include a 90-foot misty waterfall near Ash Cave at Hocking Hills State Park, near Columbus. In the northeast, at Cuyahoga Valley National Park, Brandywine Falls cascades for about 67 feet.

These fishermen hope to catch trout at the Rocky River Reservation in Cleveland.

A 90-foot waterfall tumbles over Ash Cave, Ohio's largest recess cave.

DISTINCT SEASONS

Ohio has four well-marked seasons. Salem native and nature-lover John Paul Tolson finds something special in each one: "Autumn's orange-yellow leaf glow, the hush after a deep winter snowfall, spring rivers running fast and steely clear, and black raspberries glistening in summer's sun." Ohioans may complain about the state's severe winters, but some miss these seasons once they move away. "I never did get used to year-round sun," said a twenty-two-year-old who left Ohio to attend college in southern California. "It felt strange not to see snow or notice big changes from season to season."

Winters can be harsh in northeast Ohio, which receives most of the state's annual 2.5 feet of snow. Geauga County, east of Cleveland, averages nearly 9 feet of snow per year. "The snow can be beautiful to look at, though I don't enjoy driving in it," said Lillian Galchick, who lives in Columbiana County. Sometimes the snowfall is so heavy that it completely covers cars parked on the street.

Spring, often brief, is usually rainy. About 38 inches of precipitation fall each year. Summer brings thunderstorms, often severe ones. Ohio lies on the eastern edge of America's Tornado Belt, and generally a few twisters strike the state each year. A deadly tornado struck Lorain in June 1924, killing eighty-five people and injuring one thousand others. It destroyed two hundred stores and five hundred homes in the region. In 1985 a tornado outbreak in northeastern Ohio killed twelve people and struck four hundred homes and other buildings, causing millions of dollars worth of damage. During the warm months, daisies, black-eyed Susans, violets, honeysuckle, Queen Anne's lace, and sunflowers grow wild in meadows, woods, and lawns.

In the fall tree leaves change from green to dazzling shades of red, orange, gold, yellow, and violet. Many adult Ohioans fondly recall leaves

A WOOLLY WINTER?

While neighboring Pennsylvania looks to the groundhog to predict the weather, Ohioans rely on a caterpillar. At the Woolly Bear Festival in Vermilion each October, people examine the woolly bear caterpillar's black and reddish brown stripes to see what kind of winter lies ahead. It is said that more black color means that cold and blizzards are coming, and thinner black stripes promise milder weather. A parade, a costume contest, and caterpillar races are among the other attractions at this annual festival in northern Ohio.

crunching underfoot as they walked to school, the fun of jumping into leaf piles, and the scent of burning leaves at sunset. Autumn is also the time for high school football games, hayrides, county fairs, hundreds of festivals, and trips to local farms to pick apples and pumpkins.

Autumn in Ohio is ablaze with color at Wayne National Forest.

PROTECTING FORESTS AND WILDLIFE

Conservation groups have worked to protect certain forested areas from being cut down. Some of these areas are now designated as state parks. Protecting the forests also protects many animal habitats. As forests have been cut down, more animals have become threatened or endangered.

In 1993 a team was organized to save the endangered Karner blue butterfly, which had last been seen in Ohio in 1988. A population of these butterflies lived in oak savannas in a small part of northwestern Ohio. Wildfires and land development in the area destroyed much of their habitat and caused the loss of wild lupine, which is the only plant that these butterflies eat when they are caterpillars. Government agencies, butterfly experts, and conservation organizations worked together on the Ohio Karner Blue Butterfly Recovery Team.

The Karner blue butterfly is an endangered species in Ohio.

In 1998 the Toledo Zoo began breeding Karner blue butterflies that came from a population in Michigan. The Butterfly Conservation Initiative met at the Toledo Zoo in 2002 to make further plans to protect the butterflies and their habitat. As of 2003 they had released more than 1,300 butterflies into the Kitty Todd Preserve, located in Lucas County, southwest of Toledo. This preserve contains black oak savanna, which is endangered around the world.

The Toledo Zoo continues to monitor the progress of the butterflies. The zoo received the North American Conservation Award in 2003 for its work in aiding three endangered butterflies, including the Karner blue. Efforts to increase the butterfly population continue. In 2006, for example, the U.S. Fish and Wildlife Service granted funds to a landowner in Defiance County for the restoration of 20 acres of black oak savanna and 30 acres of wet forest and swamp forest. As Karner blue butterflies reproduce, more people will have a chance to admire them at the preserve, along with other rare butterflies and the state-endangered lark sparrow.

Thousands of bald eagles once lived in Ohio, but by 1979 only four nesting pairs could be found there. The Ohio Division of Wildlife set up a recovery plan. This plan included efforts to educate the public about the eagles. A ban against the use of DDT, a poisonous substance once used in pesticides, also helped. The wildlife service protected nests and tried to rehabilitate injured eagles. They placed eaglets from captive breeding programs into nests where the mother eagle's own eggs had failed to hatch. By 2003 eighty-eight pairs of nesting eagles were found in Ohio. By 2005 the wildlife division reported 122 nests in thirty-nine counties. The program continues with promising results. Citizens have helped to pay for this program by buying a special Ohio Bald Eagle license plate.

A breeding program has increased the bald eagle population in Ohio.

Conservation efforts can also benefit the economy. Each year millions of tourists visit places in the United States where they can observe wildlife in a natural setting. In 2004, for example, tourism at the Ottawa National Wildlife Refuge in Oak Harbor brought $4.3 million in economic activity to hotels, restaurants, and other businesses in that part of northern Ohio.

TROUBLED WATERS

Ohio began as a farming colony, but then large cities grew along waterways where industry and shipping flourished. As Ohio's population grew and its industry prospered, the state's land and water suffered. Factories sent dirty smoke into the air. Chemical wastes, such as ash, acid, and cyanide, ran into streams and rivers. Other factories dumped oil, metals, and poisons from inks and dyes. Disease-causing organisms from sewage plants also fouled the water.

By 1948 the Ohio River was so dirty that people were not allowed to swim in it. The Cuyahoga River looked and smelled awful, too. It was strewn with steelmaking waste products, sewage, trash, and chemical wastes. For years oil had floated on the river's surface. This situation alarmed many people, especially when the Cuyahoga became the first river in the world that was officially declared a fire hazard. In June 1969 the river did indeed catch fire. Flames devoured two bridges in Cleveland, and some people began calling the city the Mistake by the Lake.

Lake Erie was filthy. Algae grew so thick that it used up the oxygen fish needed to live. The algae on the lake's surface also blocked out sunlight, so underwater plants could not grow. "By the 1960s, Lake Erie was unofficially proclaimed 'dead' . . . the air at times stank with dead fish," wrote historian Charles E. Cobb Jr. Of all the Great Lakes, Lake Erie is the most shallow. It also produces more fish for food than the other four Great Lakes combined. But fish from polluted waters were considered unfit to eat.

The Environmental Protection Agency demanded that Ohio improve its waste disposal systems, especially along the rivers. New laws set high fines for companies that did not properly dispose of their wastes. Strict laws were passed to prevent factories and sewage plants from ruining the water. Gradually, these efforts paid off. Bass returned to Lake Erie, and swimming and fishing resumed.

A new action plan was initiated late in 2004. A presidential order said that state officials, federal agencies, businesses, and scientists must work together to reduce pollution. In December 2005 Ohio Governor Bob Taft signed a resolution that launched a historic plan to support the Great Lakes. The plan provided for $20 billion in funding from various agencies and private companies. This money is being used to clean up sewage and restore wetlands. Said Keith Dimoff, deputy director of the Ohio Environmental Council, "The region's leading scientists are alarmed at the urgency of the problems facing the Great Lakes, and we need to act now to restore balance to Lake Erie and protect our drinking water, our beaches, our economy, our quality of life."

As of 2006 about thirteen million people depended on Lake Erie as a source for drinking water. The lake remained important for shipping, supporting farming, and producing energy. This new Great Lakes Restoration Plan offered great hopes for the future of Lake Erie and the other Great Lakes.

While Ohio continues to deal with pollution and other environmental matters, it also strives to maintain healthy industries. It takes hard work to maintain this balance, protecting both the environment and the economy. But hard work is a mainstay of Ohioans today, just as it was of the pioneers who settled this once rough land.

Chapter Two
Building Ohio

People have lived in what is now Ohio since at least 13,000 B.C.E. They settled first in the southeastern part of the state. Warmer temperatures after the Ice Age allowed more kinds of vegetation to grow. This provided food for the large animals hunted by the area's inhabitants, who spread north and west. These prehistoric people, called Paleoindians, often lived in caves so they could follow the animals. They also gathered nuts and berries for food. As the glaciers moved north, the mammoths and mastodons died out and the ancient peoples disappeared.

ANCIENT HUNTERS AND FARMERS

By about 7000 B.C.E. descendants of the Paleoindians, called the Archaic People, were living in the region. They lived in groups, formed villages along rivers where they fished and hunted animals for food, and used stones to make tools for hunting. Archaeologists have discovered flint-tipped spears deep in the ground where the Archaic People once built their homes. They also found charcoal, which shows that these people used fire. Some buried their dead in gravel hills called kames and they are known as Glacial Kame Indians.

Ohio's growth was spurred on by the thousands of emigrants who settled its land.

A new era called the Woodland Period began about 900 B.C.E. and lasted about two thousand years. The people who inhabited present-day Ohio during the Early Woodland Period lived mostly around rivers in the southeast. Known as the Adena, they left behind mounds that offer a glimpse of their lifestyle. Carvings found in these mounds show what the people themselves might have looked like. The remains of their homes show that their dwellings were circular in shape. Scientists have unearthed objects made of copper, clay, and stone from these ancient sites. The Adena pipe, one of the oldest Ohio artifacts found in good condition, dates back to about 100 B.C.E. Copper was not common in Ohio, so these people must have traded with other groups. Adena artifacts have also been found in Vermont and other states.

Between 100 B.C.E. and 600 C.E. the Hopewell people formed villages and hunted and gathered for their food. They lived in the northern part of present-day Ohio as well as in the south along various rivers. In mounds built by the Hopewell, scientists have dug up articles made from obsidian, a hard glassy rock that comes from volcanoes. Other objects also show that these people traded with others who lived thousands of miles away. They may have exchanged flint for other materials. The amazing mounds they built show high levels of skill in measuring the land and marking out the shapes they wished to make, including octagons.

Around 1000 C.E. the Hopewell were gone and a new cultural group appeared. They lived in a structure built by the Hopewell that became known as Fort Ancient, a name historians have also given to this group. Their culture is much like the culture of Native Americans who lived in Mexico. It's possible that the Hopewell migrated north from Mexico to what is now the United States. The Native Americans known as the Shawnee may have descended from this group.

These groups also built mounds. More than ten thousand mounds of different sizes have been found in Ohio. While some are burial grounds, others are made in geometric or animal shapes. These mounds may have been used for religious ceremonies. The Great Serpent Mound near Peebles in southern Ohio is the largest, most complex mound in the United States. It dates back to around 1000–1200 C.E. Formed of stone and yellow clay, it is an amazing 1,335 feet long and looks like a huge snake.

When European settlers arrived in the 1600s, they did not see many settled groups of Native Americans. Conflicts with the powerful Iroquois tribe that dominated the region that includes present-day New York had crushed the Erie Indians. By the 1650s Iroquois warriors had attacked and destroyed dozens of Erie villages in order to control their hunting and beaver-trapping grounds. Some settlers came into the Ohio country to hunt, gather food, or trap furs. By the 1700s, however, Native Americans

The Giant Serpent Mound is more than 1,300 feet long, 4 to 5 feet high, and 20 to 25 feet wide, making it the largest of its kind.

were living in settled villages where they were growing crops, as well as hunting and gathering. The largest group, the Shawnee, lived in the Ohio Valley. The Miami, Wyandot (also called Huron), Mingo, Delaware, Ottawa, and Chippewa were also dispersed around the region. These groups are known as historic tribes because European explorers and settlers recorded information about them.

Many Indian villages were located near river valleys in central and southern Ohio, where people found ample opportunity to fish and to raise corn, squash, sunflowers, pumpkins, beans, and tobacco. They hunted deer, rabbit, bear, wild turkey, and other animals. They also traded with Native-American groups living as far away as the Gulf of Mexico and the Rocky Mountains. Travelers communicated with each other by marking symbols on trees along the trails they used.

Many Native Americans of Ohio settled along rivers where they could easily fish and trade.

EUROPEANS ARRIVE

The French explorer René-Robert Cavelier, Sieur de La Salle is the first European known to have entered the Ohio region. In 1669 and 1670 La Salle sailed the Ohio River and was amazed by the beauty of the region. He called the river *la belle rivière,* "the beautiful river." Based on La Salle's travels, France claimed all the land between the Great Lakes and the Ohio River valley.

Fur trappers from both France and England soon descended on the area. Traders gave Native Americans knives, axes, metal pots, cloth, woolen blankets, beads, guns, and gunpowder in exchange for the pelts of beaver, bear, otter, fox, and raccoon.

During the 1700s both the British and the French claimed territory in Ohio. France controlled the lower Ohio River valley and set up trading posts

Native Americans bring furs to trade with the Europeans.

to control the fur trade. Conflicts over land led to open warfare beginning in 1754, when the French and their Native-American allies fought the British in what became known as the French and Indian War. When Britain won the war in 1763, it gained control of all of Ohio.

In 1772 a group of Moravian missionaries from Pennsylvania and Native Americans who had converted to Christianity founded the first organized settlement in Ohio. Schoenbrunn (German for "beautiful spring") Village was built on the bank of the Tuscarawas River near present-day New Philadelphia. These newcomers hunted, fished, and farmed the fertile land of the Ohio River valley. Their village thrived for five years but was abandoned during the Revolutionary War.

RUGGED PIONEERS

While England ruled the American colonies, it banned settlement west of the Appalachian Mountains. That changed after the colonists won the Revolutionary War in 1783 and became independent. The new United States claimed all the land east of the Mississippi River that England once held.

Soon, settlers began trickling into Ohio. A group of men from New England formed the Ohio Company of Associates to buy land in Ohio. In 1788, on the Ohio River at the mouth of the Muskingum River, they established Marietta (named after Queen Marie Antoinette of France), the first permanent white community in Ohio, which became a prosperous port city.

Established in 1788, Marietta, Ohio, was the first permanent settlement in the Northwest Territory.

Other settlers headed west in sturdy covered wagons, making their way down muddy trails and across swollen rivers to get to the new territory. Some settlers were misled by land dealers who showed them pictures of developed towns where, in fact, there were only dirt trails. Newspaper ads claimed that Ohio land was "of a much better quality than any other known to New England people." Soon, "Ohio fever" was sweeping the East Coast.

THE HAT ON THE SWAMP

In the early days of Ohio, many a traveler grumbled about the terrible roads. Tired men shared woeful tales about how they had made their way across dirt trails, ruts, and rivers only to find themselves in a muddy swamp. One traveler told a swamp tale to top them all:

While carefully crossing a deep swamp, he had seen a fine beaver hat lying in the mud. What's that? he wondered.

Just then, the hat moved. Though the traveler was startled, he was too curious to flee. Instead, he poked the hat with his horsewhip. The hat fell off, revealing a man's head. The man looked up at the traveler, smiled, and said, "How do you do?"

The traveler realized that the fellow was up to his neck in mud, and he apologized for having knocked off the hat. "Perhaps I can pull you out from the mire?" he offered.

"Oh, don't worry," said the other. "It's true that I'm in quite a predicament, but my horse is right here beneath me. Together, we've managed to get through worse roads than this."

Although land was cheap, surviving on it was difficult. Settlers struggled against the sometimes severe weather as well as the bears, wolves, and weasels that attacked their farm animals. Many pioneers died from malaria and other diseases. But the region provided a good life for those who could handle it. The wild territory contained plenty of game for skilled hunters. "The deer were so plentiful that they seemed to look out from the woods . . . to see what we were about," wrote one newcomer in 1835. And the rich soil proved bountiful for the hardy pioneers.

One of the hardest tasks was clearing the wooded land of trees to make room to plant crops. The trees were chopped down, and then the stumps were either burned out, pulled out with the help of oxen, or left to rot away. Frequently, settlers were forced to plant seeds among the dying tree trunks because there was no time to completely clear the land the first year. In 1839 one traveler wrote that the dying trees, "often scathed with fire and standing in vast numbers among the growing grain," gave "an air of bleakness and desolation to the farm lands." But finally the land was truly cleared. During the early 1800s an Ohioan described the joy of tilling cleared land: "None but those who have held the first plow, amid roots, stumps, stones, and trees, while the faithful team was pulling and jerking it along . . . can really enjoy the delight that the same plowman feels while holding the plow as it moves along without a root or stump to obstruct it."

The pioneers who settled Ohio were rugged and hardworking. They made their own soap, candles, and clothes, and transformed wood, brick, and stone into homes and barns. People united for stump clearings and quilting bees. Children also pitched in. They gathered firewood, water, nuts, and wild grapes and berries. They helped to prepare food, milk cows, and churn butter. Life was still difficult, however. Early settlers struggled to survive and "make do" without goods and services that were scarce or unavailable.

Early settlers in Ohio work together clearing the land to build their homestead.

Life in this new territory also had its pleasures. Children had fun swimming and playing outdoors, pitching horseshoes, and running footraces. Parents used whatever was available to make their children toys. Dolls were fashioned out of cornhusks, sometimes with heads made of dried apples. Deerskin stuffed with grass became a rag doll. The Native Americans showed the pioneers how to make a toy called the bull roarer from string and a stick of wood. Children swung the toy around until it made a roaring noise.

CONFLICTS WITH NATIVE AMERICANS

As news of the fertile land spread back east, whites streamed into Ohio. Native Americans, fearful of losing their land, cried, "White man shall not plant corn north of the Ohio River!" But this was not to be.

Treaties were made, then later broken by the whites. Native Americans went hungry as whites killed game on their land. As the number of white settlers in Ohio increased, violent conflicts between the newcomers and Native Americans became inevitable.

Several major battles between whites and Native Americans took place in Ohio. A Miami warrior named Little Turtle defeated American troops twice, in 1790 and 1791. In the second battle six hundred whites died, while the Indians lost only twenty-one men. But the fight over the land south of the Ohio River was not over. In 1794 the Native Americans were defeated at Fallen Timbers by U.S. troops led by General "Mad Anthony" Wayne.

The Native Americans had been relying on supplies and other help from the British to fight the Americans. After the Battle of Fallen Timbers, the

General Anthony Wayne's troops fight the Native Americans at the Battle at Fallen Timbers.

British withdrew their support. With no hope of victory, the Ohio tribes signed the Treaty of Greenville in 1795, giving up much of their ancestral lands to the United States. They continued to live on reservations in Ohio.

Early in the 1800s the Shawnee leader Tecumseh tried to unite groups of Native Americans. In 1811 he warned their leaders, "The annihilation of our race is at hand unless we unite in one common cause against the common foe." He said, "Where today is the Pequod? Where the Narragansetts, the Mohawks, Pacannokets, and many other once powerful tribes of our race? They have vanished before the [greed] and oppression of the white men, as snow before a summer sun."

Despite Tecumseh's efforts, the Shawnee and other tribes lost their ancestral lands. He died in 1813 while fighting with British troops against Americans at the Battle of the Thames in Ontario, Canada. By 1814 most Native Americans had been driven out of Ohio.

GROWTH OF A STATE

In 1803 Ohio became the seventeenth state. During the following decades Ohio would develop the excellent transportation networks that helped it become an economic powerhouse.

In 1796 Ebenezer Zane had built a road from the Ohio River opposite Wheeling, Virginia (now West Virginia), across southeastern Ohio. This road, called Zane's Trace, was the first highway leading west and for some time was the only road in the Midwest. Between 1811 and 1840 workers improved Zane's Trace, leveling it and covering it with crushed stones. It became part of what was known as the National Road. This new road made it much easier for travelers to reach Ohio, particularly by stagecoach, which hadn't been able to make it over the rough terrain of the earlier trails.

"DON'T GIVE UP THE SHIP"

During the War of 1812 the United States battled Great Britain for control of Lake Erie. In 1813 U.S. Navy lieutenant Oliver Hazard Perry was told to remove British warships from the lake.

That August Perry left Presque Isle with nine ships led by the *Lawrence*. On September 10, while anchored not far from present-day Sandusky, he spotted six British warships. Shots rang out, and Perry urged his men closer. The Battle of Lake Erie was fierce and bloody. More than one hundred of the *Lawrence*'s 130 crew members were killed or wounded. The sails were shot to shreds. Perry left the *Lawrence* in a rowboat and made his way to another ship, where he raised a large blue banner that read, "Don't Give Up the Ship!"

Soon, the tide turned for the Americans. Expecting Perry to surrender, British ships came closer and two of them collided. The wind also shifted to favor the Americans. Perry opened fire on the British, and they were eventually forced to surrender. Then he sent his now-famous message, written on the back of an envelope, to U.S. Army general William Henry Harrison: "We have met the enemy and they are ours." This amazing victory raised the spirits of U.S. troops at a critical time in the war.

The growth of canals boosted the regional economy. The Ohio and Erie Canal opened in 1832, connecting the Ohio River and Lake Erie. From Lake Erie, goods could be shipped through the Erie Canal, down the Hudson River to the Atlantic Ocean, and then all over the world. Many other canals in Ohio also linked important rivers to each other and to Lake Erie. As business owners earned more profits, they invested in other ventures, including railroads. Railroads also helped open up Ohio. The first steam locomotive in northern Ohio was chartered in 1830. By 1860 Ohio had 2,946 miles of track, more than any other state. Many railroads were linked to canals.

Technological innovations helped improve transportation. Steamships replaced flatboats and keelboats that had to be rowed or poled. In 1818 the first steamboat on Lake Erie, *Walk-in-the-Water*, left Buffalo, New York, and arrived in Cleveland amid much fanfare. The boat could travel 8 to 10 miles per hour, carrying one hundred passengers and 300 tons of freight.

Canals opened trading in the Midwest, sparking the economy and the growth of new towns.

THE LOVELY OHIO

Twenty years after the Erie Canal officially opened in 1825, Ohio had climbed from the thirteenth to the third most heavily populated state in the Union. The newly accessible land watered by the "lovely Ohio" had tempted many.

Come all ye brisk young fel-lows,___ who have a mind to roam,___ All

in some for - eign coun - ter - ee, a long way from home;___ All

in some for - eign coun - ter - ee a - long with me to go, And we'll

Come all you pretty fair maids, spin us some yarn
To make us some nice clothing to keep ourselves warm,
For you can knit and sew, my loves, while we do reap and mow,
When we settle on the banks of the lovely Ohio.

There are fishes in the river, just fitted for our use.
There's tall and lofty sugar cane that will give to us its juice,
There's every kind of game, my boys, also the buck and doe,
When we settle on the banks of the lovely Ohio.

As Ohio's transportation networks improved, its small communities grew into thriving cities. Cleveland began as a frontier outpost. In 1796 Moses Cleaveland led a group from Connecticut to map out a city where the Cuyahoga River meets Lake Erie. Although Cleaveland never returned to Ohio, the new settlement took on his name, losing the first *a*. A magazine article in 1853 praised the city's attractions: "So extensive is the lake that it has all the grandeur of an ocean view. The harbor of Cleveland is one of the best on the lake, being spacious and safe and sufficiently easy of access." Cleveland eventually grew into a major transportation and industrial hub.

In southern Ohio, Cincinnati became a center for shipping, manufacturing, and, particularly, meatpacking. So much pork was packed and shipped in Cincinnati—400,000 hogs every year—that the city was

During the mid-1800s Cincinnati thrived as a shipping and manufacturing port.

nicknamed Porkopolis. By the 1850s it was America's sixth-largest city. Much of the state was experiencing similar growth. In 1800 only 45,000 people lived in Ohio. By 1850 the population had skyrocketed to nearly two million, making it the nation's third most populous state.

THE FIGHT AGAINST SLAVERY

During the mid-1800s Ohio became embroiled in the bitter arguments over slavery that divided the North and South. Most Ohioans, especially those in the northern part of the state, opposed it. Ohio was home to many leading abolitionists—people who wanted to abolish slavery. In Mount Pleasant, Charles Osborn started the *Philanthropist*, America's first antislavery newspaper, in 1817. Another important abolitionist newspaper, the *Anti-Slavery Bugle*, came out of the northeastern Ohio towns of Salem and New Lisbon. Newspapers such as these were just the beginning of Ohio's development into a center of abolitionism. By the late 1830s more than two hundred antislavery societies were at work in Ohio, including one in Portage County with more than nine hundred members, which claimed to be the largest in the country.

In southern Ohio, however, more people bought and sold goods with people living in slave states across the Ohio River. These states included Kentucky and Virginia. Despite these differences, most Ohioans wanted to preserve the Union. They opposed the idea of southern states leaving the United States to form a separate government.

In 1850 Congress passed the Fugitive Slave Act, which required federal agents to help slave owners track down escaped slaves. Many Ohioans bitterly opposed this law. Congressman Joshua Reed Giddings said, "Let the President drench our land of freedom in blood, but he will never make us obey that law."

Indeed, many Ohioans instead tried to help slaves escape. Ohio was the site of hundreds of stations on the Underground Railroad, a network of hiding places for people fleeing slavery in the South. More than 40,000 of the estimated 100,000 runaways used the Ohio route, making it the busiest "line" on the railroad. Levi Coffin, who hid slaves in his home near Cincinnati, was regarded as the Underground Railroad's unofficial president.

Oberlin in northern Ohio was another famous station. In 1858 several townspeople and Oberlin College students were arrested for aiding a runaway slave. They willingly went to jail to draw attention to their cause. While they were in prison, friendly jailers let them publish an antislavery paper. After they were freed, a crowd of supporters and a brass band welcomed them home.

Ohio played an important part in the Union effort after the Civil War began in 1861. About 320,000 Ohioans served in the Union Army. One of the most famous was ten-year-old Johnny Clem of Newark, who made his name as the Drummer Boy of Shiloh, the youngest military drummer in the country.

Ohio contributed far more than just men to the war effort. Ohio factories produced muskets, cannons, uniforms, shoes, tents, and saddles. Its packing plants sent meat and lard to the hungry troops. Families kept farms running while the men were away.

Running away from his Ohio home before his tenth birthday, Johnny Clem joined the 22nd Massachusetts regiment, which adopted him as its mascot and drummer.

POPULATION GROWTH: 1810–2000

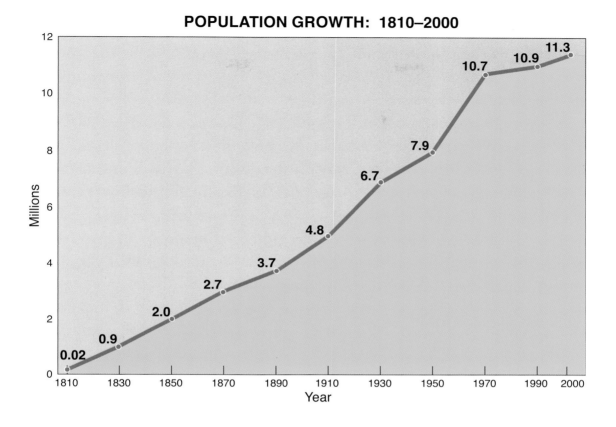

BOOM AND BUST

After the North won the Civil War, Ohio continued to prosper. Iron and steel industries thrived in Cleveland, which lay close to large coal beds. Ships brought limestone from Lake Huron and iron ore from Lake Superior. Glass and clay production boomed.

Industrial jobs drew immigrants to Ohio from all over Europe as well as from other states. But while many business owners grew wealthy, workers generally earned low wages for hard, often risky, jobs. Those who became sick, injured, or jobless had no security.

To improve their lot, workers began joining labor unions. The American Federation of Labor was established in 1886 in Columbus, Ohio. The United Mine Workers of America was formed in Columbus five years later. Laws began to regulate big business and give workers more rights.

In 1913 an old pioneer route that crossed northern Ohio was chosen to become part of the historic Lincoln Highway. This road ran from New York City to San Francisco and was the first road to connect the two coasts. Renamed Highway 30 in 1926, this road enabled people to move goods more easily, which encouraged the economy.

Ohio's economy continued to thrive into the 1920s. But then, in 1929, the Great Depression hit. Ohio was devastated. Factory orders plunged and businesses shut down. By 1932, 37 percent of Ohioans were out of work. In Cleveland and other cities, banks failed. People could not withdraw their savings, and businesses could not meet payrolls. By 1935 the unemployment rates in some cities soared to 80 percent. Many farmers lost their land as food prices fell below the cost of production.

Ohioans did whatever they could to survive. Many grew their own food and made their own clothing and other household goods. A senior citizen who grew up in Flushing, Ohio, recalls, "Mom made our clothes, often out of flour sacks. She unraveled adult-size sweaters and used the yarn to knit mittens and scarves for us kids. Our big garden kept us going. We canned so many fruits and vegetables, even wild mushrooms and weeds. But we did have to go to the relief center for things like flour." Soup kitchens opened in cities and small towns to feed the state's many unemployed people. Relatives and friends shared cramped housing to avoid homelessness.

The unemployed line up for soup and bread in Cleveland during the Great Depression.

In the face of such hardships, many Ohioans welcomed Franklin Roosevelt's New Deal. After winning the 1932 presidential election, Roosevelt launched massive programs to help people survive the depression. Government-run projects put millions back to work building dams, bridges, public buildings, and roads.

But only with the outbreak of World War II did the economy really recover. About 840,000 Ohioans served in the armed forces during the war. While men fought overseas, Ohio women worked in defense plants and factories. Ohio turned out planes, automobiles, and trucks, as well as rubber and steel, for the war effort.

RECENT CHALLENGES

The 1960s and 1970s were stormy times for the whole nation. The civil rights movement made more people aware of racism in America. Violent riots erupted in Hough, the inner-city section of Cleveland, as African Americans expressed frustration over decades of inequality.

Bitter arguments raged during the 1960s over America's involvement in the Vietnam War. Many young people, in particular, opposed the war. In May 1970 antiwar protests at Kent State University near Akron turned violent. On the evening of Friday, May 1, some students who went to the downtown area broke windows and threw bottles at police cars. The next day town officials imposed a curfew and Kent students were ordered to stay on campus. About two thousand protesters gathered around the Reserve Officer's Training Corps building that evening, and some unknown persons set the building on fire. By Sunday Ohio National Guard troops occupied Kent's campus. Another large crowd of more than 1,500 gathered on Monday, some as protesters and others as spectators. When crowd members

National Guardsman fire tear gas into a crowd at Kent State University in May 1970.

ignored orders to disperse, guardsmen fired shots, killing four students and wounding nine others. The tragedy at Kent State shook the nation.

The 1970s saw a slump in the Ohio economy, caused by foreign competition, outdated equipment, and less demand for heavy industry. Many factories moved to warmer places in the South, which often didn't have unions, allowing companies to pay workers less and avoid restrictive "work rules." This slump continued through the last decades of the twentieth century. Between 2001 and 2006 the state lost 200,000 manufacturing jobs.

Ohio has been working to update its industries, develop new ones, and attract businesses from foreign countries and other states. During the 1990s the number of new jobs increased and unemployment rates declined. By 2000, however, global competition, particulary from China with its low-cost labor force, had wiped out these gains. In 2003 Governor Bob Taft said, "We're in a new economic era. Traditional industries have departed, are declining or are severely threatened. We've lost thousands of traditional manufacturing jobs over the last ten years. And unfortunately, many of these jobs are not coming back." After he was elected governor in November 2006, Ted Strickland said that one of his top priorities was to create more living-wage jobs.

Political leaders have disagreed about the best ways to solve the serious economic problems that the state was facing in the early twenty-first century: should they seek changes in the international trade policies that are made in Washington, D.C.? Strengthen the state's education system and provide more aid for college students? Impose fewer regulations on businesses and lower their taxes? Some experts say that the state must once again become a leader in new ideas. Inventions and development of new businesses drove the state's economy during the twentieth century. That same creativity and "idea-making" could build a more promising future.

Chapter Three

Life in the Buckeye State

Buckeyes who move away often recall Ohio fondly. At a party in New York City, some well-known Ohioans were heaping praise on their home state. An exasperated New Yorker asked, "If Ohio's such a great state, why didn't all of you stay there?" Author James Thurber, one of the Ohioans present, replied, "Well, you see, out there the competition is too tough."

AN ALL-AMERICAN STATE

In 1803 Ohio became the first "all-American state," settled by people from every state that already existed. Few of these people were aristocrats. Hard work, practical ideas, and neighborliness meant more in the wilderness than social class. Most Ohioans today are, likewise, middle class.

Ohio is average in other ways as well. Much like the nation as a whole, the state's population is about 85 percent white and 12 percent African American. During the 1990s more Asians, particularly from India, arrived.

Most people who call Ohio home are born in the United States.

By 2005 Asians made up 2 percent of the population. These new citizens had come from India, China, Japan, Korea, Vietnam, and the Philippines. More Hispanics also moved to Ohio during the 1990s and made up 2 percent of the population as of 2005. Most previously lived in Mexico or Puerto Rico.

Like all Americans, Ohioans move around more than they once did. This often happens because they change jobs or relocate after they finish college. A seventy-seven-year-old woman in Salem remarked, "When my children were growing up, we had the same families on our block for twenty years. Now we seem to have a new neighbor or two every few years. Young people don't stay in their hometowns like they used to."

Hispanic girls celebrate their heritage at the Circle Parade at Cleveland University.

ETHNIC OHIO

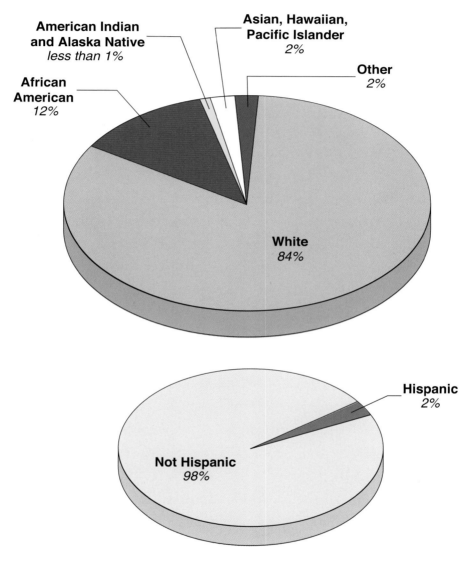

American Indian and Alaska Native
less than 1%

Asian, Hawaiian, Pacific Islander
2%

Other
2%

African American
12%

White
84%

Hispanic
2%

Not Hispanic
98%

Note: A person of Cuban, Mexican, Puerto Rican, South or Central American, or other Spanish culture or origin, regardless of race, is defined as Hispanic.

FROM MANY LANDS

Although today nearly 97 percent of Ohioans were born in the United States, once people came from all over the world to work in Ohio. Irish, Swedes, and Norwegians helped build canals and railroads or took jobs as dockworkers. Italians, Poles, Germans, and Welsh manned the mines and iron and steel industries or worked in sausage factories or meatpacking plants. Wave upon wave of immigrants came to Ohio—from Russia, Lithuania, Croatia, Slovenia, Serbia, Greece, Romania, Czechoslovakia, and Hungary. These immigrants mined coal and worked on farms. Some of them started bakeries, candy shops, shoe stores, hardware stores, and other businesses. Others worked as craftsmen or skilled laborers.

The diverse origins of Ohio's people are evident in the names of its cities: Dublin, New Paris, Dresden, Geneva, Toledo, Holland, Oxford, Warsaw. As of 2005 the largest ancestry group in the state was German, which made up about 25 percent of the population. Next came Irish (12 percent), African American (12 percent), and English (9 percent).

Today, the cultural influence of these diverse immigrants can still be seen in Ohio. For example, Ohio has the largest population of Hungarian Americans of any state, and more Hungarian Americans live in Cleveland than in any other city. It is home to a Hungarian-language newspaper and several of the finest Hungarian restaurants in America. On the menu are popular dishes such as goulash (a meat dish seasoned with paprika) and palascinta (thin pancakes served with preserves).

Ohio also has the largest Slovenian population outside of Slovenia. As of 2005, 80,000 Slovenian Americans were living in Cleveland. This community is known for a famous musician, Grammy Award winner Frankie Yankovic, called "the Polka King." The National Cleveland-Style Polka Hall of Fame celebrates Yankovic and other aspects of this kind of music. People in Cleveland's Slovenian-American community publish a newspaper and gather for political and cultural events. Towns in northeastern Ohio also have Slovak clubs for people of Slovenian ancestry.

A traditional Hungarian dance is performed by the Zivili Dance and Music Troupe from Ohio.

During the 1990s and the early years of the twenty-first century, more than 30,000 Somali refugees moved to Columbus, Ohio. These immigrants escaped from their war-torn country in Africa. By 2006 they arrived in central Ohio at a rate of about thirty people per day. As a result, Columbus has the second-largest population of Somali people in any U.S. city. Somalis have become active members of the community as workers, business owners, students, and homeowners. Many of them are mothers whose husbands were killed or who were separated from their husbands because of the war. The city's social service agencies worked to help them adjust to their new homes and gave them information about health care, schools, and other services.

Somali girls attend the fifth grade at Highland Avenue Elementary School in Columbus.

AFRICAN AMERICANS

African Americans have lived in Ohio since its early days. Many came by way of the Underground Railroad. Thousands more came to Ohio for its job opportunities and found work in factories and defense plants. Ohio also offered educational opportunities. Wilberforce University near Dayton, founded in 1856, was the nation's first private university operated by African Americans with a mostly African-American student body.

As of 1870 African-American men in the state were eligible to vote, and some served in the state legislature. One of them, newspaper publisher Harry Smith, helped to pass a law that banned racial discrimination in public places.

African Americans celebrate their culture and heritage at the Jubilation Celebration in Ohio.

The Ohio Accommodations Law of 1884 banned discrimination based on race. Even so, African Americans did face racism and discrimination in education, jobs, and housing. They also faced new threats after the reformed Ku Klux Klan moved into northern states after 1915. Klan members were active in some parts of Ohio during the 1920s.

By the 1900s most of Ohio's African Americans lived in cities, notably Cleveland. They formed the first Ohio chapter of the National Association for the Advancement of Colored People there in 1912.

As the civil rights movement gained ground during the 1950s and 1960s, opportunities expanded for African Americans. The state legislature created the Ohio Civil Rights Commission in 1959. The commission had the power to enforce laws that banned discrimination on the basis of race. The federal Civil Rights Act of 1964 put more legal protections in place and brought more attention to problems stemming from racism.

By the mid-1960s more African Americans were being elected to office in Ohio. Robert C. Henry became mayor of Springfield in 1966, although just 14 percent of the voters were African American. In 1967 former state legislator Carl Stokes became mayor of Cleveland, making him the first African American elected to head a major city. While serving in that office, Stokes stressed ways to improve housing and jobs for people in the city. Stokes later became a journalist and the U.S. ambassador to the Seychelles, an island nation in the Indian Ocean. In 2002 the city dedicated its Stokes Federal Courthouse in his honor.

Today, African Americans continue to increase their presence in all walks of life, from politics to courtrooms to boardrooms to universities. A mathematics professor who grew up in Ohio said, "When I began college [in Cleveland in 1959], there weren't many black faculty members. That has changed a great deal."

Carl B. Stokes was the first African American to be elected mayor of a major city.

DIVERSE RELIGIONS

"A church around every corner" is how one Ohioan described her hometown of 14,000 people. "People here are religious but they respect other people's beliefs."

Early settlers from New England brought their Congregationalist religious beliefs with them to Ohio. By the 1800s other Protestant groups, including Episcopalians, Presbyterians, Universalists, Baptists, and Methodists, lived in the state. Ohio became an odd mix. Quiet towns with strict laws that forbade drinking alcohol or doing business on Sunday existed near riverboat towns famous for dancing, gambling, and horse racing.

A number of small religious groups, including the Amish, Shakers, Moravians, Zoarites, and Quakers, came to Ohio. Today, more Amish live in Ohio than in any other state. Traditional Amish families still live much as their ancestors did more than a century ago, without motor vehicles, electricity, televisions, or telephones. They wear simple dark clothing and hats or head coverings. These families make most of the things they need and use. Their horse-drawn buggies can be seen on back roads, mostly in the northeastern and east-central part of the state.

Holmes County is home to the world's largest concentration of Amish settlements.

The North Union Society of Shakers built a settlement in 1822 in the present-day Cleveland suburb of Shaker Heights. They believed in hard work, simplicity, and thrift. Men and women lived apart, and belongings were shared by all. The Shakers farmed and operated a sawmill, woolen mill, tannery, linseed oil mill, and broom factory. The community lasted until 1889.

Many Catholics and Jews also came to Ohio. In 1826 the first Catholic church in Cleveland was organized. Catholic immigrants from Ireland, Italy, Poland, and other countries found factory jobs in small towns and cities. Today, Roman Catholics are the single largest religious group in Ohio. Cleveland's first Jewish synagogue was completed in 1846. In Cincinnati in 1875, Hebrew Union College, with its Jewish Institute of Religion, became the first center of Jewish higher learning in the United States.

SEEKING RELIGIOUS FREEDOM

Numerous religious groups fleeing persecution in Europe made their way to Ohio. Among them were about two hundred Protestant separatists known as the Zoar Society. They came from Germany where they had been persecuted for criticizing the Lutheran Church, the dominant religious group in the region. By 1817 the Zoarites had settled in northeastern Ohio. These immigrants earned money to pay for the land by working on the Erie Canal, which ran from New York into Ohio. They built a communal society, sharing with each other whatever they grew and produced. They named their community Zoar, after a town of refuge in the Old Testament. The Zoarites built homes and barns, along with a tannery, brickyard, ore furnace, and workshops. Zoar was one of the first and most successful religious communal societies in America. It lasted for eighty years.

Historic Zoar Village has been restored and is open to the public. An 1850s-style harvest festival is held there each August. Besides music and good food, the festival includes displays of folk arts and crafts, antique carriages, and classic cars. Christmas in Zoar features strolling carolers, German holiday food, and tours of decorated homes.

Large Jewish congregations also grew in Columbus and Cincinnati and still flourish in all three cities today. Northeastern Ohio is also home to many Muslims, and recent Asian immigrants have brought their Buddhist, Shinto, and Hindu traditions to the state. The city of Westerville had one of the first Shinto shrines in the continental United States.

POPULATION DENSITY

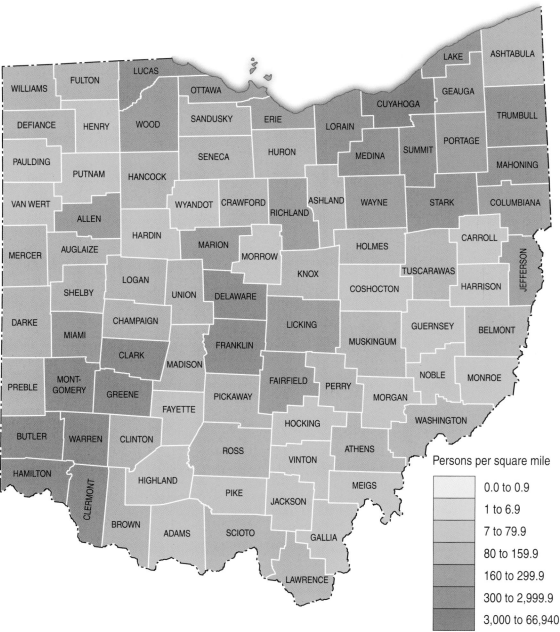

Persons per square mile

- 0.0 to 0.9
- 1 to 6.9
- 7 to 79.9
- 80 to 159.9
- 160 to 299.9
- 300 to 2,999.9
- 3,000 to 66,940

CHALLENGES FOR CITIES

Ohio cities, like other cities across America, have struggled with poverty, unemployment, crime, and crowded, run-down schools with high dropout rates. During the economic slump of the 1970s, many businesses shut down, which meant less tax money for services such as schools and health care. As such problems multiplied, many people who could afford to do so left the cities for the suburbs. Between 1950 and 1990 Cleveland's population fell 44 percent.

Although the economy improved somewhat during the 1990s, another slump occurred as the twenty-first century began. Overseas competition meant that workers in other countries could produce many manufactured goods more cheaply. When state and local communities are left with a lower tax base, they must make difficult choices about funding their programs.

Elected officials have tried to deal with these problems as well as other issues that affect the quality of life. When U.S. Senator George Voinovich was mayor of Cleveland from 1979 to 1988, he promoted various kinds of partnerships between government and industry to try to improve the city and keep people there. School-to-work programs helped high school students move into the workforce by giving them on-the-job training while they were still in school. Students in cities and outlying suburbs took part in joint musical events and other activities. Voinovich's administration also worked to clean the air and water.

To the south, the city of Columbus has benefited from a fairly diverse economic base and efforts to revitalize downtown streets and neighborhoods. Columbus has faced the challenges of absorbing refugees who must adjust to life in a new country. Thousands of people from Somalia, Ethiopia, and Eritrea have settled in this city. Some were living in other states but moved to Ohio because other people from their homelands found Columbus to be a welcoming community. Many refugees are also waiting for their loved ones to join them in Ohio. They have asked the government for help in releasing their family members from camps overseas where they are waiting for permission to come to the United States. Said Columbus mayor Michael B. Coleman, "The cultural, educational, health-care and employment barriers for these new Americans are enormous [but] in Columbus, we embrace and extend our hands to everyone."

One major step for these new Americans was to learn English. In fall 2004 about 1,120 Somali students entered the Columbus public school system and some spent time at welcome centers taking English lessons. It had cost the school district nearly $10 million in 2003 to provide introductory English classes. The county received $1.2 million in federal funds in 2004 to help provide for some of the refugees' needs.

ROADS TO LEARNING

The earliest settlers built schools along with their homes and churches. They erected one-room log or stone schoolhouses wherever there were enough children. Parents gave money or goods to pay the teacher, who often roomed with a local family. In 1825 public schools were established. Public high schools sprang up around 1850.

Ohio's colleges and universities are among the world's finest. One of the best known of its public institutions is The Ohio State University (OSU) in Columbus. In 1878 William H. Scott, an early president of the university, said, "The University will be a glory to the state, a light and an inspiration to all who value and seek after the things of the mind." OSU is now one of the largest universities in the world, with a main campus that

Founded in 1870, Ohio State University is the largest university in the United States.

serves about 50,000 students. *U.S. News & World Report* magazine has ranked it among the top twenty public universities in the United States.

Dennis Mardas, a stockbroker who has lived in Columbus since 1959, noted "the number of small and large colleges in our area, aside from Ohio State." He said, "In the past, people in other regions may have perceived Columbus as a 'cowtown.' But we have grown to be a business center, and most of all, an education town." Today, half a million students are enrolled at Ohio's more than 130 colleges and universities. They include a variety of large, medium, and small schools throughout the state.

One of the most renowned is Oberlin College in northern Ohio. Two years after it opened in 1833, Oberlin was the only school in the country where men and women of any race could apply. In 1855 John M. Langston, an African-American graduate of Oberlin, became clerk of an Ohio township, which made him the first African American in the United States to hold elected office. The school is especially well known for its music programs.

In Yellow Springs, Antioch College has been known for its individualized approaches to learning and programs that involve community service and active involvement in social issues. One famous alumna is the late Coretta Scott King, wife of Dr. Martin Luther King Jr.

SPORTS CRAZY

It seems that Ohioans have always loved sports. In 1893 Mount Union College was one of the first American colleges to form a basketball team. The Canton Bulldogs were one of the earliest football teams. In 1869 the Cincinnati Red Stockings became the first professional baseball team. They traveled 11,877 miles in one season, playing any team that challenged them. Their official record that year was fifty-seven wins and no losses. The team's proud manager said that the sport had not only provided entertainment but had also boosted pride in the city.

When the first professional baseball league, the National Association (later the National League), was formed in 1871, the season opened in Cleveland. Today, Ohio baseball fans continue to cheer on the Cincinnati Reds and the Cleveland Indians. The Indians excited fans when they won the American League pennant in 1995 and went to the World Series for the first time since 1954, losing to the Atlanta Braves (4–2). They won the American League title again in 1997 and played, but lost, in the World Series. From 1995 to 1999, and again in 2001, they won the American League Central Division title. Another historic moment for the team came in 1947 when Larry Doby became the first African-American player in the American League.

A Cleveland Indians fan awaits the opening pitch at Jacobs Field.

Basketball is another popular sport. The Cleveland Cavaliers play in the National Basketball Association. Columbus has its Cyclones, who play in the International Basketball League.

Football fans root for the Cincinnati Bengals and pack the stadium at OSU, where the Buckeyes are a perennial college powerhouse. During the 1970s the Buckeyes became the first Big Ten team to play in four consecutive Rose Bowl games.

A RACE JUST FOR KIDS

Each year in late July, Akron, Ohio, hosts the All-American Soap Box Derby. Young people between the ages of eight and seventeen from around the United States and from other countries compete in this downhill race, which is held at Akron's Derby Downs racetrack.

The Soap Box Derby began in 1934 during the Great Depression. Young people used wooden crates that had contained boxes of soap to build their cars. Today, they can buy approved kits that can be assembled into racers. Strict standards regulate the size, weight, and cost of the cars.

Between three and four hundred contestants usually take part each year, driving their homemade, engineless cars that are powered by gravity down the hill. Winners receive college scholarships and other prizes.

In 1994 Ohioan Danielle Del Ferraro, age thirteen, became the first two-time winner in the history of the derby. She won the Masters division, after having triumphed in the Kit division the previous year. For the first time, in 2001, a Japanese contestant took part in the race. At the 2006 races two Ohioans placed in the top six in their divisions: Dennis VanFossen of Barberton (Stock) and Alexandria Terrigno of Campbell (Masters).

Other sports have been gaining fans in the Buckeye State. A new hockey arena was built in downtown Columbus for the National Hockey League's Blue Jackets. The city also has a major league soccer team, the Columbus Crew. In 1999 a $28 million stadium was opened about 4 miles out of town to house games featuring the Crew and their opponents.

FAIRS AND FESTIVALS

Want to see a Mohican powwow, a mock Civil War battle, a Slavic folk dance, Scottish bagpipers, a hydroplane race, or a motorcycle rodeo? Would you like to pitch horseshoes, stomp grapes, or stir apple butter over an open fire? Taste a zucchini milkshake or pumpkin taffy? You can do all this and more at the fairs and festivals held in Ohio. These events celebrate the history, ethnic roots, and special features of each locale.

Many Ohio festivals focus on food—everything from corn, apples, and strawberries to honey, black walnuts, and walleyes. Circleville, near Columbus, is renowned for its annual fall Pumpkin Show. More than 100,000 pounds of pumpkins, gourds, and squashes are on display. Bands serenade visitors as they applaud magic acts, admire arts and crafts, and view the "world's largest pumpkin pie." In 2006 this pie contained 795 pounds of cooked pumpkin. Among the many pumpkin snacks are muffins, cakes, cookies, candies, ice cream, and more than 100,000 donuts. The Ohio Honey Festival is held in August in Hamilton. More than two hundred booths offer samples of various kinds of honey for sale. During the festival a beekeeper amazes visitors by creating a "living bee beard" on his face. A seven-year-old who saw the bee beard said, "I couldn't believe that was *really* bees until I saw him close up and they were!"

FRIED APPLES

After the Civil War a group of Ohio women wrote *The Buckeye Cook Book* (1876) for "Plucky Housewives Who Master Their Work Instead of Allowing It to Master Them." The book includes recipes for such delicacies as skunk and raccoon. More typical is this tasty and simple dessert. Ask a grown-up to help you with this recipe.

Oil or shortening
Firm apples, cored, and cut into 1-inch-thick wedges (or, to be fancy, 2-inch-thick rings)
Brown or white sugar
Cinnamon (optional)

Put enough oil or shortening in a frying pan to just cover the bottom. Over low to medium heat, fry the apple slices until they are tender. Remove from heat and place on serving dish. Sprinkle with sugar or a combination of sugar and cinnamon.

Festivals also celebrate the diverse cultures that enrich Ohio. The Puerto Rican Cultural Festival takes place in Cleveland each summer. The Slavic Village Harvest Festival, also in Cleveland, features a kielbasa (a type of sausage) cook-off. Sugarcreek is the site of the Ohio Swiss Festival. Alpine charm and Swiss-style buildings attract visitors to this city year-round. The festival features music, costumed dancers, traditional foods, a Swiss wrestling match, and a stone-tossing contest.

Each fall Kirtland holds the Vintage Ohio Wine Festival. Visitors can tour local wineries and watch wine-making contests. In their bare feet people can stomp barrels filled with grapes. The Geneva Grape Jamboree in Geneva located on Lake Erie, also celebrates the local harvest with music, dancing, parades, contests, tours of wineries, grape stomping, and displays of grape products.

Besides attending such festivals, Ohioans can be found enjoying themselves at church suppers, school picnics, city street fairs, Fourth of July parades, and other community gatherings. "You can have your fancy balls and opening nights," said one native Ohioan. "For me, this is where the real fun is."

Chapter Four

Middle of the Road

An old adage says, "As Ohio goes, so goes the nation." This adage often comes up when people talk about presidential elections, since Ohio has voted for the losing candidate only twice in the past 104 years. Opinions in Ohio tend to reflect those around the United States. Professional pollsters call Ohio a "barometer state," a place to find out how Americans feel about political and social issues.

INSIDE GOVERNMENT

Although in the frontier days Ohio's state government was small and limited in scope, today it plays an active role in business, education, the environment, tourism, and other areas. Like the federal system, the Ohio government has three branches: executive, legislative, and judicial.

Executive

The top state official is the governor, who is elected to a four-year term. A governor may serve up to two four-year terms. He or she proposes an annual budget, appoints people to key positions, and directs executive agencies and committees. Other elected state officials include

The house of representatives and senate meet at the Ohio Statehouse in Columbus.

73

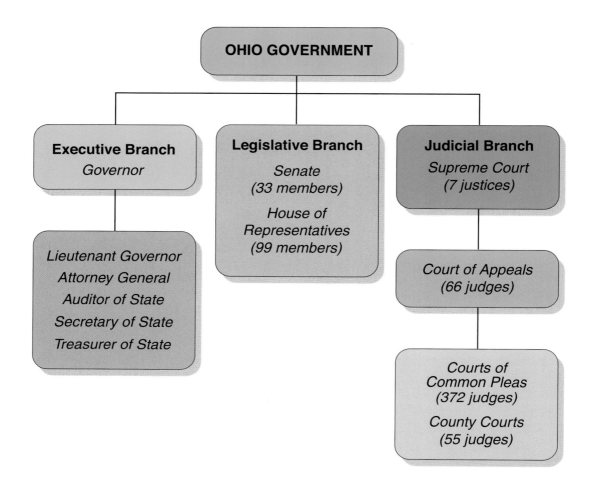

OHIO GOVERNMENT

Executive Branch
Governor

Lieutenant Governor
Attorney General
Auditor of State
Secretary of State
Treasurer of State

Legislative Branch
Senate
(33 members)

House of
Representatives
(99 members)

Judicial Branch
Supreme Court
(7 justices)

Court of Appeals
(66 judges)

Courts of
Common Pleas
(372 judges)

County Courts
(55 judges)

lieutenant governor (who takes over if the governor dies or cannot serve), secretary of state, attorney general, auditor, and state treasurer.

Legislative

The general assembly is Ohio's lawmaking body. It includes a senate with thirty-three members who serve four-year terms, and a house of representatives with ninety-nine members serving two-year terms. The general assembly creates and changes laws and approves the annual state budget.

The highest state law is the Ohio Constitution. The state legislature can propose amendments to the constitution. Amendments can also be proposed by voter initiative or a constitutional convention. A majority of voters in a general election must then approve the amendment for it to be enacted.

Judicial

The highest state court is the Ohio Supreme Court, which is made up of a chief justice and six associate justices who are elected to six-year terms. The state has twelve courts of appeal, which are also headed by judges serving six-year terms.

Ohio has eighty-eight courts of common pleas, one for each county. In addition, there are county courts, municipal courts in larger cities, probate courts, and juvenile courts.

MOTHER OF PRESIDENTS

Ohio has sometimes been called the Mother of Presidents because seven U.S. presidents were born there; an eighth, William Henry Harrison, lived there most of his life. Harrison became president in 1841 and died just a month after his inauguration.

Ohio native Ulysses S. Grant, the general of the Union Army during the Civil War, became president in 1869. When he left office in 1877 he was succeeded by another Ohioan, Rutherford B. Hayes, who was replaced by yet another Ohioan, James A. Garfield, in 1881. A self-made man, Garfield had once worked guiding mules along the Ohio Erie Canal and driving boats to and from coal mines from Pennsylvania to Cleveland. Garfield was shot four months after he took office and died two months later.

Benjamin Harrison, a native of North Bend, Ohio, who entered the White House in 1889, began the tradition of the White House Christmas tree. William McKinley, from Niles, Ohio, became president in 1897.

Six months after he began his second term in 1901, he was assassinated. McKinley's love of red carnations led Ohio legislators to make them the state flower.

Cincinnatian William Howard Taft was the first president to drive an automobile. A baseball lover, he started the tradition of having the president throw the first pitch at the season's opening game. In 1921 Taft also became the only former president to serve as a U.S. Supreme Court chief justice.

The most recent Ohio president, Warren G. Harding, took office in 1921. Harding was the first president to address the American people over the radio.

One Ohioan made history as the first woman to run for president. Victoria Claflin Woodhull of Homer, a suffragist and co-owner of a stock brokerage firm, ran in 1872 on the Equal Rights Party ticket. During the 1870s another Ohioan, James Royce of Newark, became president of the West African nation of Liberia.

American reformer Victoria Claflin Woodhull was the first woman ever to run for the presidency of the United States.

FIGHTING CRIME

Like many other states, Ohio has been striving to reduce crime rates and make streets and schools safe for citizens. Generally, people in small towns feel safer than people in large urban areas. A resident of the small town of Sebring said, "I don't worry much about crime, although it can happen anywhere. There's never been an incident in our neighborhood." City dwellers, on the other hand, sometimes suffer greatly from their area's high crime rates. In 2005 Youngstown had the fourth highest murder rate in the nation: 43.7 per 100,000 people, compared to a national rate of 5.6. Cleveland and Cincinnati ranked in the top fifty cities in the United States with the highest crime rates.

City schools saw rising crime rates during the 1980s, mostly drug related. "At times, we have had police officers on school grounds, and we have monitors patrolling the halls," said a teacher at a Cleveland high school. Many urban schools have had similar problems, although violent crimes decreased slightly during the late 1990s. School safety remained a problem early in the twenty-first century, primarily in urban areas.

State and local lawmakers have looked for effective ways to address drug abuse. After the 1990s more emphasis was placed on rehabilitation. Lawmakers explored the idea of sending first-time offenders caught with small amounts of drugs to rehabilitation programs rather than jail. They also reexamined laws that seemed to penalize people caught with small amounts of drugs as severely as drug dealers. Prevention through education remains a top priority since most people seeking treatment for drug abuse are under the age of twenty-five.

Ohio's police force strives to keep the state free of crime and drugs.

During the 1990s some communities participated in a federal program called COPS—Community Oriented Policing Services. Under this program police officers spend entire shifts working with the community without having to leave to answer distress calls. The program was intended to build relationships between officers and their communities and to enable officers to work on prevention. The Federal Bureau of Investigation has been working with the COPS program in Cleveland to reduce crime, drug abuse, hate groups, and gang activity.

Another program called C.O.P.—Citizen Observer Patrol—involves local volunteers who alert police to situations that need their attention. In Cincinnati this program, called the Citizens on Patrol Program, began with three neighborhoods in 1997. By 2006 it had expanded into twenty-two neighborhoods. Citizen patrols often help the police during special community events, such as holiday fireworks.

To combat crime Ohio has created stricter sentencing laws for repeat offenders. During 2004 a survey of several cities—Toledo, Columbus, Cleveland, Dayton, and Akron—showed a slight decline in crime rates. Throughout the nation the number of violent crimes went down 1.2 percent.

In 2004 the state legislature appointed a commission to examine the death penalty system in Ohio. The panel was asked to determine whether people on death row received adequate legal help during their trials and whether the cases were resolved fairly. They also looked at ways to minimize delays in the process of trials and appeals. This bill had support from both Democrats and Republicans. The death penalty was made legal again in the state in 1999 after being banned in 1963. During the first ten months of 2006, five convicted murderers were put to death by lethal injection.

OHIO BY COUNTY

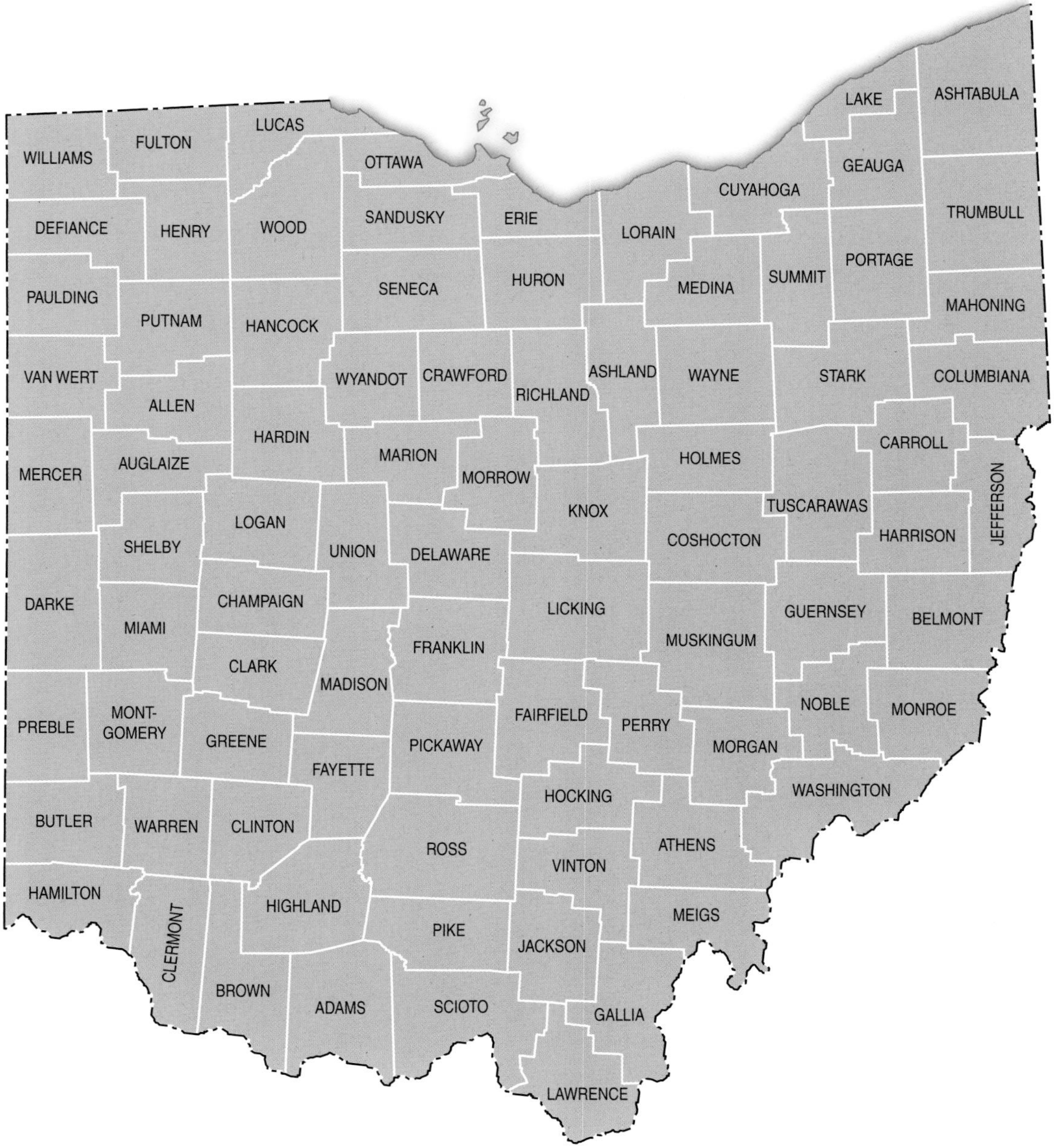

INFLUENTIAL VOTERS

In terms of party politics, Ohio seems to be evenly divided among Democrats, Republicans, and Independents, and candidates work hard to win their votes. The results on election day can be surprising. When people vote in the primaries to nominate candidates, they can request a Democratic or Republican ballot, depending on their party registration. In general elections Ohioans sometimes send one party's candidates to the U.S. Congress while voting the opposing party's candidates into the statehouse—or vice versa.

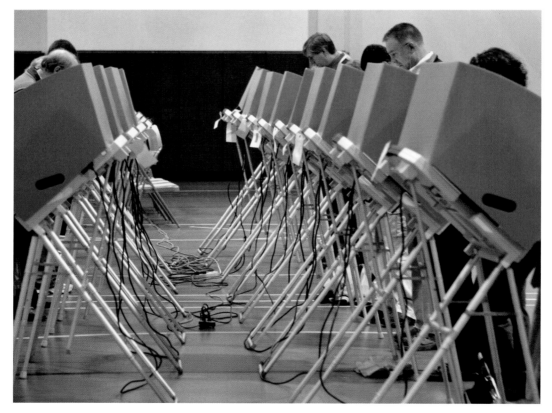

Voters take to the polls during the 2006 elections.

Ohio was in the national spotlight before and during the 2004 presidential election when candidates of both parties courted voters in this "swing state." President George W. Bush won the state with a 2 percent margin, but critics questioned the results. After the election, voters in certain urban areas complained that they had been prevented from casting their votes. Urban areas had strongly favored Senator John Kerry, the Democratic candidate, while voters in many smaller towns, especially in the southern part of Ohio, had favored Bush. Investigators looked into these charges and did not find clear evidence of wrongdoing.

It was clear that presidential candidates would again vigorously pursue Ohio's twenty electoral votes during the 2008 election. By 2006 more than a dozen potential presidential candidates had visited the state. Both Democrats and Republicans were making appearances at colleges, town meetings, and at campaign events where they supported their party's candidate in state and local elections. "Ohio is a battle-ground," said Senator John Kerry. "You can't sit around and wait. Ohioans made a huge difference last time, they could have made the whole difference. That isn't lost on anyone."

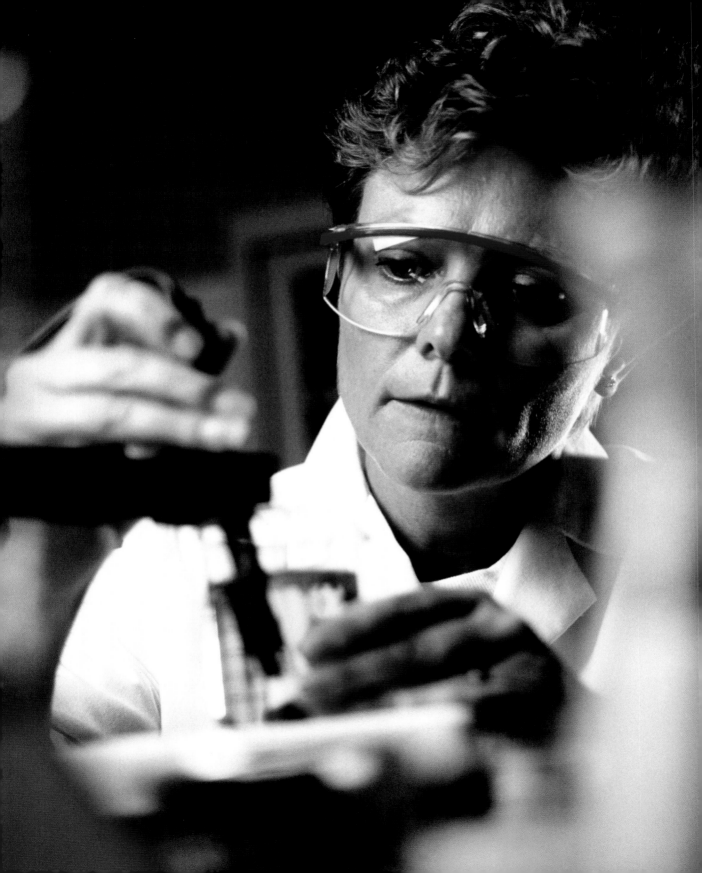

Chapter Five
Growing the Economy

During the economic slump that began in the late 1960s, Ohio's once-busy factories sat empty, their machinery rusting. The auto, steel, and rubber industries were lagging. People called Ohio and the surrounding region the Rust Belt. As plants closed down, people lost jobs or were laid off. In some cases they had worked at these plants all their lives. People who could not find another job left for other states where the job market was more promising.

This slump continued into the twenty-first century, with slight improvements during the 1990s. The loss of manufacturing jobs in Ohio, especially in the northeast, persists, and that region lost 30,000 jobs in 2002 alone. Competition from China, Japan, Korea, Germany, and Mexico had the most impact during these years. By the late 1990s global competition wiped out the job gains Ohio saw during the 1990s. Unemployment rates rose again and wages fell.

As a result, the gross state product resulting from goods-producing industries (manufacturing, farming, construction, mining, and other natural resources) has fallen. Between 1997 and 2004 it dropped by more than

Technological advances give rise to a growing industry in Ohio.

2004 GROSS STATE PRODUCT: $425 Million

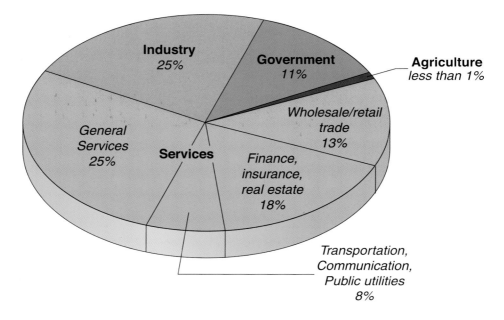

Industry
25%

Government
11%

Agriculture
less than 1%

General
Services
25%

Services

Wholesale/retail
trade
13%

Finance,
insurance,
real estate
18%

Transportation,
Communication,
Public utilities
8%

$9 billion, which was the largest decline in any state. To deal with the changing economic conditions, companies have made changes on their own, and state and local governments have looked for solutions. Like people in other states, they have had to adapt to a changing and global marketplace.

MANUFACTURING IN THE TWENTY-FIRST CENTURY

Ohio was once a manufacturing giant, and manufacturing is still important in the state. Ohio ranks second among the fifty states in steel manufacturing and processing, with a production of about 11.9 metric tons in 2003. Cheap steel imports have caused a loss of jobs in the steel industry, however. That leads to the loss of other jobs in related industries, such as companies that make steel-manufacturing equipment, or limestone mining, which is used for iron smelting.

Steel manufacturing is an important industry in Ohio, ranking second in production in the country.

Ohio's representatives to Congress have introduced bills to limit steel imports and promote practices that guarantee fair trade. Senator Mike DeWine expressed his concern that the Chinese government was subsidizing its steel industry in ways that violated free trade rules, such as tax incentives and cash and land grants. DeWine said that he was a strong supporter of free trade and open markets, but noted that "the cornerstone of truly free trade is that everyone plays by a common set of rules." A bill that DeWine introduced in 2000 became law. It provides assistance to steel-working companies in Ohio to help level the playing field as they compete with imported steel.

The state ranks second to Michigan in producing cars and trucks and first in household appliances. There are more than 330 auto-related industries in the northeastern part of the state alone. Other factories turn out many things people use every day at work or at home—car parts, chemicals, electronics, paper products, leather goods, paint, silverware, scientific instruments, and furniture. Factories in Cincinnati make more playing cards and soap than any other place in the world. The publishing and printing industries are also strong.

Only one other state, Michigan, produces more vehicles than Ohio.

Improving productivity helps some companies to thrive. For example, a company in Cleveland that makes industrial cutting tools added new technology to increase production. As a result, the manager was able to add five new employees to the company's twenty-five-person shop. Other companies have updated their equipment for the same reason.

Ohio manufacturers have become more diversified, and new service industries have developed. "We looked for new products that were in demand and have found new markets for our products," said a Youngstown plant manager. Although Akron was once almost exclusively associated with rubber making, today the city is a center for the trucking industry as well as a leading producer of ultralight aircraft.

Well-paying jobs in manufacturing call for a steady supply of qualified workers. The Northeast Ohio Manufacturing Awareness Council works to inform young people about careers in manufacturing and link them with the appropriate training programs. Some of these job-training programs are built into the high school curriculum.

MINING

Mining still plays an important part in the state's economy. Ohio is the seventh-largest coal producer in the nation. Oil, natural gas, clay, limestone, sand, gypsum, dolomite, and sandstone are also mined. Most of this sandstone is used for glassmaking. Ohio produces about 30 percent of the limestone used for building in the United States.

As of 2005 sixty-five mines operating in thirty-two counties were producing clay and/or shale for a total of about 2 million metric tons. Much of this clay was used to make certain kinds of bricks as well as pottery and tiles. Salt is also mined, but quantities produced in recent years were lower than the production levels during the twentieth century.

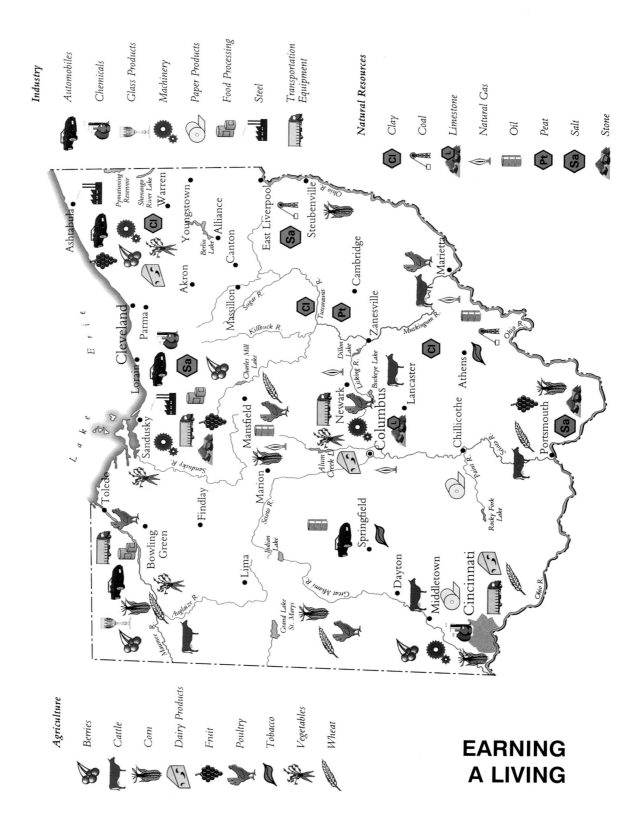

Industry
- Automobiles
- Chemicals
- Glass Products
- Machinery
- Paper Products
- Food Processing
- Steel
- Transportation Equipment

Natural Resources
- Clay
- Coal
- Limestone
- Natural Gas
- Oil
- Peat
- Salt
- Stone

Agriculture
- Berries
- Cattle
- Corn
- Dairy Products
- Fruit
- Poultry
- Tobacco
- Vegetables
- Wheat

EARNING A LIVING

FARMING

Ohio farmers have also had to adjust to changing times. "We've been farming for four generations," said a farmer in central Ohio. "Yes, it's hard these days, especially for a small operation. We make it work because we love this life." They have made their farm more profitable by growing organic produce—fruits and vegetables grown without the use of pesticides. They sell to health-food stores, vegetarian restaurants, and directly to consumers.

Today, about 3 percent of Ohioans still manage to make their living through farming. About one-third of the cropland in Ohio is devoted to corn. Corn and other grains are used for animal feed as well as foods for people around the world. Dozens of other crops are grown there, including soybeans, hay, sugar beets, tomatoes, and cucumbers. Fruits such as apples, pears, blueberries, strawberries, peaches, and sour cherries all grow well in Ohio. Excellent grapes for wine are grown on the Bass Islands in Lake Erie. Farmers also sell eggs and milk.

Although Ohio's land is fertile and well suited for farming, 3 percent of Ohioans earn their living as farmers.

OHIO WORKFORCE

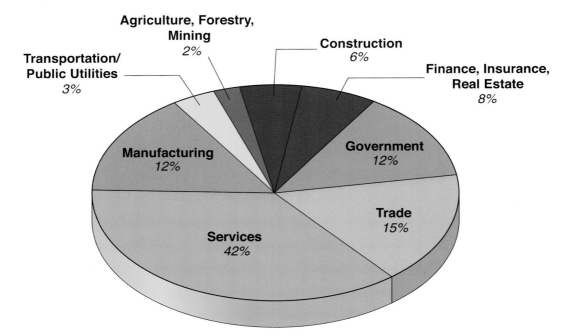

Agriculture, Forestry, Mining 2%

Construction 6%

Transportation/ Public Utilities 3%

Finance, Insurance, Real Estate 8%

Manufacturing 12%

Government 12%

Trade 15%

Services 42%

Livestock are another farm product. They include hogs and sheep. Ohio is the largest sheep-producing state east of the Mississippi River that provides quality wool products. Horses are also bred and sold out of Ohio.

Agriculture contributes more than $73 billion worth of economic activity to Ohio each year. More than eight hundred food-processing companies operate in the state, and their products are exported from as well as sold in the United States.

Ohio is now a leader in nursery stock production, providing a variety of landscaping plants and decorative plants for homes. Top crops in this area are African violets and poinsettias. The southeastern part of the state still produces lumber and wood that are used in constructing buildings and furniture. Wood from Ohio is also exported to other countries.

Ohio nursery owners take pride in their poinsettias, a top crop in the state.

TOYS AND TREATS

Young people throughout the world enjoy the toys and tasty treats that are made in Ohio. The Ohio Art Company in Bryan, near Akron, has sold more than forty million of its famous Etch A Sketches, which debuted in 1959. The Kenner Company, which produces dolls, action figures, and many other toys, is based in Cincinnati. Hudson is the home of Little Tikes, known for its toys and children's furniture. Play-Doh was also developed in Cincinnati and introduced by a company there called Rainbow Crafts.

Many popular snacks also come from Ohio. Cain's Potato Chips and Snacks Company is located in Toledo. Marion is a major producer of popping corn. The first Cracker Jack–style popcorn, as well as the first flavored chewing gum, came from the Buckeye State.

PLANNING FOR A STRONG FUTURE

As Ohioans look to the future, they believe that many new jobs might come from the scientific and technological research happening in the state. Some of this research is in the field of health care and medicine. Scientists are working on new and more powerful medical imaging techniques. Other researchers are building more sophisticated information systems. Still others are designing faster and lighter forms of aircraft. Agriculture experts are finding ways to produce more food more efficiently while still caring for the land.

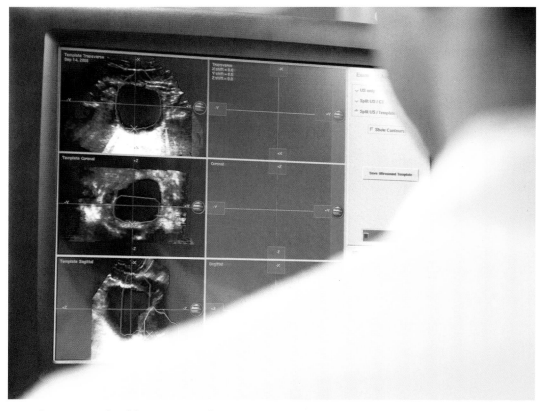

Employment in health care provides a wealth of career opportunities for Ohioans.

The ability to export more goods and products is also important. European markets account for $6 billion of Ohio's overall international exports. In recent years the state made more connections with other nations to promote trade. Governor Bob Taft led several trade trips abroad during his term in office. With a group of business leaders, he visited Japan, South America, Europe, and Mexico. These efforts have resulted in some increased business for the state. For example, in 2003 a new manufacturing plant was built by San Luis Rassini, a large, Mexican-owned automotive company, in northwestern Ohio. Two Mexican companies bought preexisting manufacturing companies in the state. One company purchased a cement plant near Dayton. One of Mexico's largest bakers, Grupo Bimbo, bought a large facility near Toledo to make tortillas and chips. These investments in local businesses provide more jobs for Ohioans.

The state hopes that more businesses will relocate to Ohio, and points out that sixty Fortune 1000 companies are already based in the state.

In recent years Ohio's leaders have declared that education and programs to strengthen families are top priorities. The state assembly made funding available so that every child in Ohio, rich or poor, could attend preschool and have access to health care. Lawmakers also considered proposals to fund programs that would make college more affordable for middle-class and lower-income families. As of 2006 Ohio ranked fortieth among the fifty states in terms of the amount of state support per student given to colleges and universities. In addition to serving children and families, programs that fund education at all levels can create healthier communities and a healthier climate for economic growth.

Strong, well-educated people—these are Ohio's most important resource. Whether they work in farming, mining, business, industry, technology or another field, it is Ohio's people who will shape the state's future.

Chapter Six
Going Far in Ohio

Ohio has something for everyone. Curious minds can explore the history of flight, pottery, or rock and roll. Thrill seekers can ride one of the world's largest roller coasters at Cedar Point or brave 6-foot-high columns of water at Tidal Wave Bay in Geauga Lake. More than sixty million nature lovers visit Ohio's seventy-four state parks each year. Travel writer Barbara Leskey tells her fellow Ohioans, "Stay where you are, and yet go far."

THE NORTHWEST

One of Ohio's most exciting regions is western Lake Erie near Sandusky and Toledo. Sandusky is the home of Cedar Point, one of the nation's largest and most popular amusement parks. It draws nearly three million guests every year. A big attraction there is the Mantis, billed as "one of the world's tallest, fastest, and steepest, standup coasters." Riders race up and down the 3,900-foot track at speeds up to 60 miles per hour. The park also features tamer rides and fun for small children. Visitors under 4 feet tall enjoy Berenstain Bear Country, with characters and buildings taken from the popular children's books. Nearby Soak City features more than a dozen water slides and other attractions on its 18-acre water park.

Young visitors study Henri Matisse's Apollo *at the Toledo Museum of Art.*

Thrill seekers get their fill at Cedar Point, one of Ohio's most popular amusement parks.

The Bass Islands draw thousands of tourists each year. Middle Bass Island features a winery in a castlelike setting. Each year barbershop quartets from around the nation gather to perform here. On neighboring South Bass is Put-in-Bay, which has a beautiful Victorian main street and a monument to Commodore Perry's famous naval victory. A Cleveland resident said, "It wouldn't be summer for us without a trip to Put-in-Bay. We bike all around, stopping to fish, hike, and to have picnics on the beach." Fishing for walleye, bass, perch, and minnies is a popular pastime here.

On Kelleys Island you can see the glacial grooves, gullies etched into the earth by glaciers 30,000 years ago. The island also has a rock inscribed with ancient Indian drawings, some of animals and others of humans smoking pipes.

Visitors view the 400-foot-long glacial groove at Kelleys Island.

TEN LARGEST CITIES

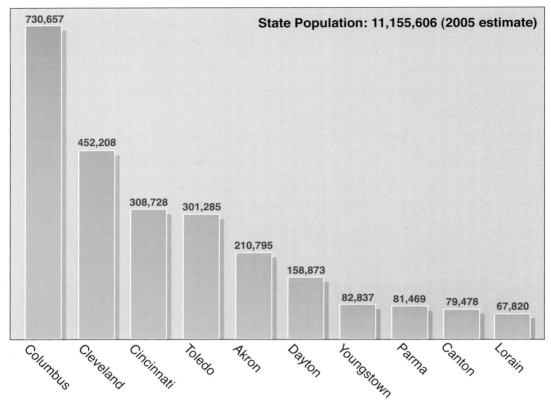

State Population: 11,155,606 (2005 estimate)

City	Population
Columbus	730,657
Cleveland	452,208
Cincinnati	308,728
Toledo	301,285
Akron	210,795
Dayton	158,873
Youngstown	82,837
Parma	81,469
Canton	79,478
Lorain	67,820

Toledo, near the Michigan border, is noted for its art museum, which houses a fine collection of ancient, American, and European art, including works by the famous European painters El Greco and Picasso. It also includes a great Egyptian collection with a real mummy.

CLEVELAND: "ONE HOT CITY"

Ohio's second-largest city celebrated its bicentennial in 1996 by calling itself "one hot city." Since then *Travel & Leisure* magazine has named it "America's 21st Century City." Cleveland features fine restaurants and cafés, shopping areas, movie palaces, and cultural attractions. Landmark buildings include the fifty-two-story Terminal Tower, Ohio's second-tallest building. From its observation deck, you can see all around the city and out over Lake Erie. The Great Lakes Science Center features many hands-on exhibits, a six-story OMNIMAX Theater, and a replica of the National Aeronautics and Space Administration mission control center in Houston.

Ohioans are proud of their outstanding cultural attractions. The Cleveland Museum of Natural History has dinosaur skeletons, bird exhibits, and a gem room full of colorful precious stones and crystals. The Cleveland Orchestra is regarded as one of the finest in the nation and the world. Visitors to the Cleveland Museum of Art can view ancient and modern works from around the globe.

With so much to offer, Cleveland bills itself as "The New American City."

FEAST OF THE FLOWERING MOON

Each May during Memorial Day weekend, Chillicothe sponsors a festival that showcases its Native-American roots and history. The Feast of the Flowering Moon, which was first held in 1984, now draws more than 80,000 people a year. Visitors can watch Native-American dancers and visit a drum maker, silversmith, bead workers, and other crafters. Some people take part in an encampment where they step back in time to the 1800s. They pitch tents near the Yoctangee River, wear nineteenth-century clothing, and cook their food over open fires. Tradesmen, blacksmiths, broom makers, and musicians add to the pioneer mood.

Other attractions include arts and crafts exhibits, contests, a Memorial Day parade, and a duck race. Many young people take part in a water race where they can use "Anything That Floats But a Boat." During the 2006 race one resourceful young man attached dozens of balloons to his canoe.

Tourists from all over the world visit Cleveland to see the Rock and Roll Hall of Fame and Museum. The museum offers visitors a chance to hear the five hundred most important rock songs of all time and learn about the artists who wrote and performed them. The collection includes musical instruments, handwritten lyrics, and other rock memorabilia, such as a guitar played by Eric Clapton and a shirt worn by Bono of U2. "Our whole family liked the hall of fame, including my grandma, who is an Elvis fan," said a teenage visitor. "You'd have to go there more than once to see everything."

A visitor from Los Angeles, California, views one of the many exhibits at the Rock and Roll Hall of Fame.

THE EAST

South of Cleveland is one of Ohio's big industrial regions. Akron is home to the Goodyear World of Rubber, where visitors learn about the material that enriched this city. Exhibits explain how rubber got its start in Charles Goodyear's kitchen, and how it has been used in everything from artificial hearts to blimps. You can even see how tires are made.

The twenty-one restored homes and buildings at Hale Farm and Village near Bath give a good idea about what life was like on an Ohio farm in the early nineteenth century. Artisans and craftspeople demonstrate glassblowing, carpentry, blacksmithing, spinning, and candle making.

Canton is home to the Pro Football Hall of Fame, which honors top players, coaches, and others who have contributed to the game. At the entrance is a statue of Jim Thorpe, an Olympic gold medalist who played for the Canton Bulldogs in the 1920s. Each summer the hall welcomes new honorees with a parade and ceremony. The Canton Classic Car Museum features more than forty beautifully restored antique cars, along with automobile memorabilia from days gone by.

South of Canton, history lives on near New Philadelphia, where the restored village of Schoenbrunn offers a glimpse

Jim Thorpe, one of the "world's greatest athletes," is immortalized at the Pro Football Hall of Fame in Canton.

of late-eighteenth-century life. Schoenbrunn began as a Christian mission for the Delaware Indians but was abandoned during the American Revolution. In 1923 the Ohio Historical Society bought the land and set out to rebuild Schoenbrunn. Today, tour guides wearing eighteenth-century dress show visitors around the village. The church and log cabins include pieces of the original buildings, as does the one-room schoolhouse, with its straight, backless wooden benches and stone fireplace. For summer visitors an outdoor drama, *The Trumpet in the Land*, tells the story of Ohio's first Christian settlement.

Life in Ohio during the 1700s is reenacted at the Schoenbrunn Village.

The Museum of Ceramics in East Liverpool examines the history of the area's pottery, porcelain, bone china, and glass industries. Each June the Tri-State Pottery Festival features pottery displays, contests, tours of local plants, antiques, and art shows.

Not far from Canton in northeastern Ohio is Amish country, a quiet farming area where people still live a simple life without many technological conveniences. The Amish towns feature shops selling homemade crafts and tools. Delicious foods can be bought at the restaurants, cheese factories, and bake shops. Visitors leave with packages of green moon cheese, maple sugar candy, and gooey shoofly pie, which has a molasses filling. Colorful handmade Amish quilts are also popular.

In Amish country it is not uncommon to see a horse-drawn buggy share the road with automobiles.

COLUMBUS

Columbus, on the east bank of the Scioto River, became Ohio's capital in 1816. The old brick and stone statehouse burned down in 1961 just as the new one was being built. The new building, which has four grand columned entrances, is one of the few state capitols that has no dome.

A great downtown attraction is the full-scale replica of the *Santa Maria*, the ship Christopher Columbus sailed to America. While you visit the boat, costumed guides tell you what life was like on the long journey across the ocean. At Ohio's Center of Science and Industry, more than one thousand exhibits make science fun. Both adults and children enjoy hands-on activities, such as hopping onto the keys of a large computer, riding a high-wire bicycle, or climbing inside a genuine 1961 Mercury space capsule.

You can also explore a model coal mine to learn about Ohio's industrial heritage.

The Franklin Park Conservatory and Chihuly Collection contain a magnificent collection of plants—more than 1,200 different kinds—from around the world and from climates ranging from desert to mountains to rain forest. Another great Columbus site offers a different way to appreciate plants. At the Topiary Garden in Old Deaf School Park, huge shrubs are trimmed to resemble people, dogs, monkeys, and even boats. Summer visitors to Columbus can refresh themselves at the Fort Rapids Indoor Waterpark Resort, featuring twelve water rides with western themes.

When in Columbus, plant enthusiasts should visit the Franklin Park Conservatory.

History can be discovered at some former stations on the Underground Railroad, which are open to the public. Among them are the Platt log cabin in West Liberty, northwest of Columbus, and the home of the Reverend John Rankin in Ripley in southern Ohio. Rankin hid hundreds of runaway slaves between 1825 and 1865. Many older homes in Ohio have secret rooms that were used to hide runaways.

Animal lovers and fans of zoologist Jack Hanna's television appearances probably know about the Columbus Zoo and Aquarium. An unusual insect collection is a featured attraction, as are the polar bears and tree kangaroos. Visitors can stop at areas designated for animals native to Asia, Africa, Australia, and North America, among others.

PLACES TO SEE

Lake Erie

Headlands Beach State Park

Ashtabula

Pymatuning Reservoir

Toledo

Cedar Point

Cleveland

The Rock and Roll Hall of Fame & Museum

Lorain

Fort Meigs

Sandusky

Parma

Sea World of Ohio

Warren

Shenango River Lake

Maumee R.

Bowling Green

Akron

Youngstown

Anglaize R.

Findlay

Berlin Lake

Alliance

Sandusky R.

Lima

Mansfield

Charles Mill Lake

Massillon

Canton

Marion

Scioto R.

Ohio's Amish Country

East Liverpool

Zoar Village

Indian Lake

Grand Lake St. Marys

Campbell Hill ▲ (1,549 ft.)

Steubenville

Tuscarawas R.

Killbuck R.

Sugar R.

Alum Creek L.

Ohio Historical Center

Newark

Dillon Lake

Cambridge

Great Miami R.

Licking R.

Zanesville

U.S. Air Force Museum

Springfield

Columbus

Buckeye Lake

The Wilds

Dayton

Lancaster

Muskingum R.

Middletown

Hocking Hills State Park

Marietta

Cincinnati

Mound City Group National Monument

Athens

Museum Center

Paint R.

Chillicothe

Rocky Fork Lake

Serpent Mound

Scioto R.

Ohio R.

Ohio R.

Portsmouth

THE SOUTH

Prehistoric mound-building cultures lived south of present-day Columbus. The Hopewell Culture National Historic Park is located near Chillicothe. People of the Hopewell culture built burial mounds at this site more than two thousand years ago. Farther south is the amazing Great Serpent Mound, which has impressed scientists from around the world. Visitors to the Leo Petroglyph site in Jackson walk along trails past a ravine to view rocks with dozens of pictures of people, birds, and animals. The meaning of these Native-American drawings remains a mystery.

Southeast of Columbus is Dayton, the birthplace of aviation. The Aviation Hall of Fame honors the scientists, inventors, pilots, and engineers who helped men and women get off the ground. The National Museum of the United States Air Force, at Wright-Patterson Air Force Base, contains the world's oldest and most complete military aviation collection. On display are B-29s, many other fighter planes, and an Apollo space capsule.

Military flying machines are on display in Dayton at the National Museum of the United States Air Force.

Farther south along the western Ohio River is Cincinnati. History lovers can sample the nineteenth century at Sharon Woods Village or examine documents and objects from the days of slavery at the Harriet Beecher Stowe Center. The Arts Consortium features an African-American museum that traces the history of blacks in the city and serves as a community arts center.

The dramatic history of firefighting is shown at the Cincinnati Fire Museum, which is located in a restored 1907 fire station. Although some people think the highlight of this museum is an 1884 steam-powered fire engine, others prefer the chance to slide down a fire pole.

The Cincinnati Zoo is the second oldest in the nation. It is famous for its comprehensive collection of wild cats—nineteen different species in all. Another highlight is its Jungle Trails rain forest exhibit, where orangutans and other primates can cavort.

The Cincinnati Art Museum has an outstanding Native-American collection as well as art from around the world. Visitors to the Cincinnati Museum of Natural History can explore a limestone cave with fossils and underground waterfalls. One contains a 30-foot waterfall and intricate mineral formations. You can also visit a simulated glacier as part of a "trip" back to the Ice Age.

Marietta, the first permanent white settlement in Ohio, is steeped in history. In this charming town you can hop on a trolley to get to the many historic homes and buildings. The Campus Martius Museum features artifacts such as furniture and tools from pioneer days. At the museum you can even amble through Ohio's oldest house and imagine how these brave settlers lived.

Visitors to Marietta can also enjoy a ride on the *Valley Gem*, one of the last stern-wheeler riverboats still operating on an inland waterway. The Ohio River Museum contains an authentic stern-wheeler, the *W. P. Snyder*, and

Charming storefronts line Front Street in historic Marietta.

other exhibits that bring to life the bygone days of the steamboat. Although another stern-wheeler, the *Becky Thatcher*, never leaves port, people flock to it anyway to enjoy a dramatic play while eating dinner.

These are just a few of the places that invite visitors to explore Ohio's history, meet famous people of the past and present, and glimpse the future while learning about science and industry. "We have some of the biggest, the best, and most beautiful things here," a proud Ohioan said of his state. "Our family has had great times right in our own backyard."

THE FLAG: The tips on the pennant-shaped flag stand for Ohio's hills and valleys, while the red and white stripes represent its roads and waterways. On the blue triangle the white circle with the red center stands for both the O in Ohio and the buckeye nut. The seventeen stars indicate that Ohio was the seventeenth state to enter the Union. The flag was adopted in 1902.

THE SEAL: The current state seal was adopted in 1996. It shows the Scioto River running between Mount Logan and a field of wheat. In the field is a bundle of seventeen arrows, again representing Ohio's place as the seventeenth state. A bundle of wheat, showing the importance of agriculture, stands next to the arrows. In the background the sun rises, casting thirteen rays over the mountain, symbolizing the original thirteen American colonies.

State Survey

Statehood: March 1, 1803

Origin of Name: Ohio is named after the Ohio River. The Iroquois Indians called the river the O-hy-o, which means "something great" or "great river."

Nickname: Buckeye State

Capital: Columbus

Motto: With God, All Things Are Possible

Mammal: White-tailed deer

Bird: Cardinal

Flower: Red carnation

Insect: Ladybug

Reptile: Black racer (snake)

Stone: Flint

Tree: Buckeye

Wildflower: White trillium

Cardinal

White trillium

BEAUTIFUL OHIO

This perennially favorite waltz was written in 1918 and adopted as the official state song in 1969. In 1989 new lyrics were composed, changing the feeling from an old-fashioned love song to an expression of affection for the whole state.

Words by Wilbert B. McBride   **Music by Mary Earl**

GEOGRAPHY

Highest Point: 1,549 feet above sea level at Campbell Hill in Logan County

Lowest Point: 455 feet above sea level at the intersection of the Ohio and Miami rivers in Hamilton County

Area: 40,953 square miles

Greatest Distance North to South: 205 miles

Greatest Distance East to West: 230 miles

Bordering States: Michigan to the north, Pennsylvania and West Virginia to the east, West Virginia and Kentucky to the south, and Indiana to the west

Hottest Recorded Temperature: 113° F at Gallipolis on July 21, 1934

Coldest Recorded Temperature: −39° F at Milligan on February 10, 1899

Average Annual Precipitation: 38 inches

Major Rivers: Auglaize, Chagrin, Cuyahoga, Grand, Great Miami, Hocking, Huron, Little Miami, Maumee, Muskingum, Ohio, Olentangy, Portage, Sandusky, Scioto, Tuscawaras, Vermilion

Major Lakes: Alum Creed, Berlin, Buckeye, Burr Oak, Caesar Creek, Dillon, Erie, Grand Lake St. Marys, Indian, Mosquito, Piedmont, Rocky Fork, Salt Fork, Seneca, Tappan

Trees: ash, beech, birch, buckeye, chestnut, cottonwood, crab apple, dogwood, elm, fir, hemlock, hickory, larch, locust, maple, oak, Osage orange, pawpaw, pine, redbud, sassafras, spruce, sumac, sweetgum, sycamore, tulip, walnut, willow

Wild Plants: aster, black-eyed Susan, bluebell, buttercup, coneflower, Dutchman's-breeches, field daisy, ginseng, goldenrod, golden seal, ironweed, jack-in-the-pulpit, lady's slippers, marsh marigold, mayapple, milkweed, mountain laurel, pitcher plant, rhododendron, shooting star, squirrel corn, sunflower, trillium, wild carrot, wild columbine, wild geranium, wild lily, wild rose, wood lily

Animals: beaver, chipmunk, coyote, eastern cottontail rabbit, gray fox, groundhog, mink, muskrat, opossum, raccoon, skunk, squirrel, weasel, white fox, white-tailed deer

Gray fox

Birds: blackbird, Canada goose, cardinal, cowbird, dove, duck, finch, grouse, gull, hawk, heron, hummingbird, mockingbird, nuthatch, owl, pheasant, sparrow, starling, swallow, swan, thrush, vulture, whippoorwill, woodpecker, wren

Fish: bluegill, carp, catfish, gar, largemouth bass, muskellunge, northern pike, perch, sheephead, smallmouth bass, sucker, sunfish, trout, walleye, white bass

Endangered Animals: bald eagle, bobcat, cave salamander, common tern, eastern plains garter snake, eastern salamander, golden-winged warbler, green salamander, Indiana bat, Kirtland's warbler, loggerhead shrike, copper-belly water snake, northern harrier, peregrine falcon, piping plover, sandhill crane

Endangered Plants: Eastern prairie fringed orchid, lakeside daisy, Northern wild monks-hood, running buffalo clover, small whorled pogonia, Virginia spiraea

Golden-winged warbler

TIMELINE

Ohio History

700 B.C.E. The Adena begin building mounds in what is today southern Ohio.

1740s B.C.E. Shawnee, Miami, Wyandot, Mingo, and Delaware live in present-day Ohio.

1669–1670 Frenchman René-Robert Cavelier, Sieur de La Salle, is the first European to see the Ohio region.

1745 The French establish the first fort in Ohio on Sandusky Bay.

1749 Celoron de Blainville of France travels through the Ohio Valley, claiming the area for his country.

1763 After its defeat in the French and Indian War, France gives up most of its territory in North America, including the Ohio region; Native Americans attack British forts along the Great Lakes, capturing the British Fort Sandusky at Pontiac's Rebellion.

1772 Moravian leader David Zeisberger founds the Schoenbrunn Village to shelter Christian Native Americans.

1773 The first school west of the Appalachian Mountains opens at Schoenbrunn.

1775 The American Revolution begins.

1787 Ohio becomes part of the Northwest Territory, which will eventually become five states.

1788 Marietta, the first permanent white settlement in Ohio, is founded.

1793 The first newspaper in the Northwest Territory, the *Centinel of the North-Western Territory*, is published in Cincinnati.

1794 At the Battle of Fallen Timbers, U.S. troops defeat Native-American forces, ending Indian resistance to settlement in Ohio.

1796 Cleveland is founded by Moses Cleaveland.

1803 Ohio becomes the seventeenth state; the first state capital is Chillicothe.

1813 During the War of 1812 American ships under the command of Lieutenant Oliver Hazard Perry defeat a British fleet in the Battle of Lake Erie near Put-in-Bay.

1816 Columbus becomes the state capital.

1835 Ohio and the Michigan Territory argue over the boundary line between the two, leading to the Toledo War.

1836 Ohio's first railroad, a horse-drawn train, operates between Toledo and Adrian, Michigan.

1845 The Miami and Erie Canal, between Cincinnati and Toledo, is completed.

1850 State women's rights convention is held in Salem in April, the first women's rights convention to be held in Ohio.

1861–1865 The Civil War is fought; more than 300,000 Ohioans fight for the Union.

1868 Civil War hero and native Ohioan Ulysses S. Grant is elected president of the United States.

1869 America's first professional baseball team, the Cincinnati Red Stockings, is formed.

1913 Some 467 people die in the worst flooding in the history of the state.

1941–1945 America fights in World War II; about 840,000 Ohio men and women serve in the armed forces.

1955 The Ohio Turnpike is completed; Cleveland Indians baseball team wins the American League title and plays in the World Series.

1967 Carl B. Stokes becomes the first African American to lead a major American city when he is elected mayor of Cleveland.

1970 National Guard troops kill four students at Kent State University during protests against the Vietnam War.

1974 A tornado kills 315 people in Xenia and destroys much of the town.

1985 Tornado outbreak injures dozens of people and destroys homes and other property in northeastern Ohio.

1995 The Rock and Roll Hall of Fame and Museum opens in Cleveland.

2004 State legislators approve a plan to establish an African American Hall of Fame honoring Ohioans; Ohio is a major battleground during the presidential election and controversy results after votes are counted.

2006 Representative Ted Strickland becomes Ohio's first Democratic governor since 1994 as Democrats sweep the midterm elections; voters pass a new law that bans smoking in workplaces, restaurants, bars, and most other indoor public places.

ECONOMY

Agricultural Products: apples, celery, corn, cucumbers, dairy products, eggs, grapes, hay, hogs, mushrooms, nursery plants, oats, onions, peaches, potatoes, poultry, rye, sheep, soybeans, strawberries, sugar beets, sweet corn, tobacco, tomatoes, wheat

Sheep

Manufactured Products: automobiles, chemicals, electrical equipment, furniture, glass products, industrial machinery, metals, paper products, processed foods, rubber products, trucks and buses, wood products

Natural Resources: clay, coal, gypsum, limestone, natural gas, peat, petroleum, salt sand and gravel, sandstone, shale

Business and Trade: communications, finance, insurance, printing and publishing, real estate, retail trade, tourism, transportation, wholesale trade

CALENDAR OF CELEBRATIONS

Sandusky Bay Ice Festival Visitors gather in January to watch iceboat races, ice-fishing, ice-sculpting, and other sports.

St. Patrick's Day Parade and Celebration What better place to be a little Irish on St. Patrick's Day than in Dublin? This central Ohio city celebrates the March holiday starting with a pancake breakfast and parade, followed by plenty of Irish food, music, and fun.

U. S. Grant's Birthday Celebration Point Pleasant and Georgetown commemorate Ulysses S. Grant's birthday in late April. During the celebration you can tour his birthplace and boyhood homes and see a reenactment of life in a Civil War camp.

The Great Fossil Hunt Held in May at Caesar Creek State Park near Waynesville, this event celebrates the area's abundant fossils. Park rangers are on hand to help you hunt for and identify the fossils of tiny sea animals.

Festival of the Fish The bounty of Lake Erie is celebrated with food and music during this June festival in Vermilion. Wacky boat races as well as an evening parade of boats are held on the Vermilion River.

Old Northwest Territory Primitive Rendezvous The explorers, pioneers, fur trappers, and Native Americans of early Ohio come to life during this June event in Piqua. Costumed actors demonstrate what it was like when frontier people came together to trade and celebrate. You can sample foods of the era and view arts and crafts demonstrations.

Great Mohican Indian Powwow Native Americans from all over the United States come together at Loudonville for this annual summer and/or fall festival. You can watch Native-American dancers, sample authentic foods, and listen to storytelling.

Dayton Air Show Considered the finest air show in the country, this July event features the very best of the aviation world. Watch the skies as pilots perform death-defying aerobatics, or stroll the grounds of the Dayton International Airport to get a close-up look at modern and historical aircraft.

Pro Football Hall of Fame Festival Canton celebrates its football heritage with a weeklong festival in July just before the new Hall of Fame members are inducted. There's a grand parade, a drum corps competition, hot air balloon flights, and lots of food. It ends with two pro teams playing in the Hall of Fame Game.

Ohio State Fair

Ohio State Fair If you like your good times to be big, you'll love the Ohio State Fair in Columbus. Every August 20,000 farm animals are brought in to compete for prizes. Besides touring the animal barns, you can check out the life-size butter sculptures in the dairy barn, enjoy thrill rides, listen to music, and eat great food.

Ohio Renaissance Festival Travel back to the days of knights and fair maidens during this festival held near Waynesville each September. At a replica of a sixteenth-century English village, you can watch jousting, archery and storytelling, sample medieval foods, and dance to minstrel music.

Ohio Swiss Festival Locally made Swiss cheese is the star at this Amish country celebration held every September in Sugarcreek. There's also Swiss music, polka dancing, sporting events, a yodeling contest, and a parade.

German Village Oktoberfest Held every fall (late September to early October) in Columbus's German Village, an authentic ninteenth-century German immigrant neighborhood, this Oktoberfest has everything you'd expect. You can fill up on German foods, from bratwursts to cream puffs, then dance to the music of oompah-pah bands.

Pumpkin Show Ever seen a pumpkin pie that's 5 feet across? How about a pumpkin that weighs over 1,000 pounds? Those are just a few of the attractions at this October festival in Circleville. You can sample pumpkin fudge or pumpkin burgers, or try your hand at the pumpkin-carving contest. The celebration also includes rides, music, and parades.

Pumpkin Show

Covered Bridge Festival The more than a dozen covered bridges near Ashtabula are celebrated every October with a parade, draft-horse pulls, a plowing contest, and covered bridge tours. There's also food and live entertainment.

International Festival Cultures from around the world are highlighted at this exciting festival. During this November celebration in Columbus, you can discover the food, music, and crafts of more than sixty nationalities.

STATE STARS

Neil Armstrong (1930–   ), of Wapakoneta, was the first person to walk on the moon. Armstrong was the commander of the *Apollo 11* mission, when he set foot on the moon on July 20, 1969, and spoke the famous words, "That's one small step for a man, one giant leap for mankind." Before he began training as an astronaut in 1962, Armstrong served as a navy pilot during the Korean War and then worked as a civilian test pilot.

Halle Berry (1966–   ) became the first African American to receive an Academy Award for best actress, which she won for her performance in the 2001 film *Monster's Ball*. This Cleveland native also received a Golden Globe award for her performance in the HBO production *Introducing Dorothy Dandridge*. A former beauty pageant winner, Berry frequently appears on lists of the world's most beautiful women.

Halle Berry

Erma Bombeck (1927–1996) earned fame for writing humorous newspaper columns on the trials of everyday life and parenthood. She also authored a number of best-selling books, including *The Grass Is Always Greener over the Septic Tank* and *If Life Is a Bowl of Cherries, What Am I Doing in the Pits?* Bombeck was born in Dayton.

Charles Chestnutt (1858–1932), a noted African-American writer, was born in Cleveland. His works often explored prejudice, and he was one of the first writers to portray blacks realistically and sensitively. Chestnutt's works included *The Conjure Woman* and *The House Behind the Cedars*.

George Armstrong Custer (1839–1876) was born in New Rumley. He first achieved fame as a Union cavalry officer during the Civil War. Following the war Custer fought against the Plains Indians and was killed during the Battle of the Little Bighorn in Montana.

Clarence Darrow (1857–1938), one of America's greatest defense lawyers, was born in Kinsman. Darrow's most famous case was the Scopes "monkey trial," in which he defended a teacher accused of teaching the theory of evolution.

Charles Gates Dawes (1865–1951), a Marietta native, spent much of his life in public service. In 1925 he won the Nobel Peace Prize for his plan to restore the economy of Germany following World War I. Dawes served as vice president of the United States under President Calvin Coolidge and as U.S. ambassador to Britain.

Rita Dove (1952–   ), of Akron, is an accomplished poet. Her poetry collection *Thomas and Beulah* won the Pulitzer Prize. In 1993 Dove became the first African American, and the youngest person ever, to be named poet laureate of the United States. Dove's father was a research chemist who broke the color line in the tire industry.

Paul Laurence Dunbar (1872–1906) earned fame for his poetry and novels, which were often written in African-American dialect. His works included *Lyrics of Lowly Life* and *The Sport of the Gods*. Dunbar was born in Dayton.

Thomas Alva Edison (1847–1931), who was born in Milan, was one of the world's greatest inventors. He was the only American inventor to hold more than one thousand patents. Edison's inventions include the electric light bulb, the phonograph, the storage battery, and the motion picture projector.

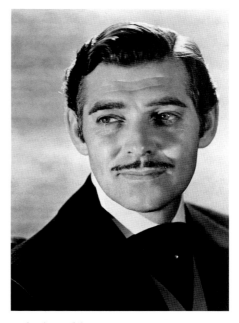

Clark Gable (1901–1960), a native of Cadiz, was a well-known movie star. He won an Academy Award for his performance in *It Happened One Night*. His most popular role was that of Rhett Butler in *Gone with the Wind*.

Clark Gable

John Glenn (1921–   ) was the first American to orbit the earth. Glenn had been a fighter pilot in both World War II and the Korean War. As a test pilot he was the first person to fly across the United States at supersonic speed. Then, in 1962, he made his brief historic flight around the earth. Later, Glenn, who was born in Cambridge, served in the U.S. Congress as a Democratic senator from Ohio from 1975 until he retired in 1998.

Ulysses S. Grant (1822–1885) was the eighteenth president of the United States. Born in Point Pleasant, Grant gained fame as a Union general during the Civil War, winning many victories along the Mississippi River, including the capture of Vicksburg, Mississippi, in 1863. He later became the commander of all Union military forces during the war.

Zane Grey (1872–1939) has been called the father of the Adult Western. His numerous novels include *Riders of the Purple Sage, Call of the Canyon*, and *The Thundering Herd*. Grey was born in Zanesville.

Scott Hamilton

Arsenio Hall (1955–   ), born in Cleveland, was the fist African American to host a successful late-night talk show. *The Arsenio Hall Show* ran from 1989 to 1994. Hall has appeared in several movies, including *Coming to America*.

Scott Hamilton (1958–   ) won the Olympic gold medal for men's figure skating in 1984 and was the men's world champion from

1981 through 1984. He performed with the Ice Capades and Stars on Ice and served as a TV commentator during major figure-skating competitions. Born in Toledo, Hamilton was raised in Bowling Green.

Bob Hope (1903–2003) moved to Cleveland at age four. Starting off in vaudeville, a style of variety entertainment, Hope went on to star in many successful comedy films, such as *Road to Singapore*, *Road to Rio*, and *Call Me Bwana*. He later hosted a series of popular television specials and was often chosen to emcee the annual Academy Awards. Hope is well known for entertaining American military forces all around the world during both peace and war.

Charles F. Kettering (1876–1958), of Loudonville, is credited with many important inventions. After creating the electric cash register, Kettering came up with his most famous invention, the electric starter for automobiles. He also invented safety glass, fast-drying automobile paint, and a fuel injection system for diesel engines. He served as the director of research for General Motors for many years.

Maya Lin (1959–   ) was only twenty-one years old when her design was chosen for the Vietnam Veterans Memorial in Washington, D.C. Her monument, a black granite wall inscribed with the names of the war's dead, is a popular and emotional attraction. The young artist, who was born in Athens, also designed the Civil Rights Memorial in Montgomery, Alabama.

Toni Morrison (1931–   ) writes about the struggles of African-American women. Her works include *Song of Solomon* and *Beloved*, which won a Pulitzer Prize in 1988. In 1993 she became the first African-American woman to receive the Nobel Prize for literature. *Beloved* tells the story of an escaped slave living in post–Civil War Ohio, while Morrison's first book, *The Bluest Eye*, was set in her northern Ohio hometown of Lorain. Morrison's novels have been praised for their brilliant language, strong emotions, and universal themes.

Paul Newman (1925–   ) is one of America's most popular movie actors. His films include *The Hustler, Cool Hand Luke, Butch Cassidy and the Sundance Kid, The Sting,* and *The Color of Money.* In recent years, Newman, who was born in Shaker Heights, has marketed a line of gourmet food items, such as salad dressing and popcorn. All profits go to charity.

Jack Nicklaus (1940–   ), a Columbus native, is one of the greatest professional golfers of all time. Although he majored in pharmacy at Ohio State University, his golfing talent led him to turn pro in 1961 after he won his second big major amateur title. Nicklaus won the Masters Tournament a record six times and the U.S. Open four times. He was elected to the World Golf Hall of Fame in 1974. Nicklaus has also designed golf courses around the world. In 1986 he won his seventy-first lifetime title in a dramatic one-stroke victory at the Masters Tournament.

Annie Oakley

Annie Oakley (1860–1926) Phoebe Anne Moses, better known as Annie Oakley, was born in a log cabin in Darke County, Ohio.

As a teenager, she began touring the country in vaudeville shows to perform her sharpshooting skills. Later, she joined Buffalo Bill's Wild West Show, astonishing audiences around the world with her sharpshooting and stunts on horseback.

Jesse Owens (1913–1980) moved to Cleveland as a young boy. As a track star at Ohio State University, he set a number of world records. In the 1936 Summer Olympics in Berlin, Germany, Owens won four gold medals in the 100-meter and 200-meter dashes, the long jump, and the men's relay. Because Owens was black, his victories embarrassed Nazi leader Adolf Hitler, who had hoped to use the Olympics as a showcase for his theories of white supremacy. Known as the Buckeye Bullet, Owens won fans over with his poise and friendliness as well as his athletic talent.

Sarah Jessica Parker (1965–   ) is a well-known actress who appeared as part of the cast in the television series *Square Pegs* and several feature films, including *The Family Stone* and *Failure to Launch*. Born in Nelsonville, she studied voice and ballet and played the lead role in the hit Broadway musical *Annie* from 1977 to 1981.

Eddie Rickenbacker (1890–1973) of Columbus was a pioneer in the development of both the automotive industry and aviation. He was a racecar driver before World War I, when he served as a combat pilot with the first U.S. air squadron ever to fight in wartime. He completed twenty-six missions and won numerous awards, including the Medal of Honor. After the war, he started an automobile company and helped to form Eastern Airlines.

Branch Rickey (1881–1965) helped to integrate baseball. In 1945, as general manager of the Brooklyn Dodgers he recruited Jackie Robinson, the first black player to play on a major league team in the twentieth century. A native of Stockdale, Rickey had once played in the minor leagues. While coaching at Ohio Wesleyan University, he was upset when hotels and restaurants would not serve first baseman Charles Thomas on road trips because he was African American. Rickey later said, "I vowed that I would always do whatever I could to see that other Americans did not have to face the bitter humiliation that was heaped on Charles Thomas."

Pete Rose (1941–   ), one of baseball's greats, was born in Cincinnati and spent much of his career with the Cincinnati Reds. As a player-manager for the Reds in 1985, he broke the all-time hitting record of 4,191 held by Ty Cobb.

William Tecumseh Sherman (1820–1891) was one of the best-known generals to emerge from the Civil War. His "March to the Sea" through Georgia in 1864 helped destroy the South's will to fight, but also caused intense bitterness among southerners. He later became the commanding general of the army. Sherman was born in Lancaster.

Steven Spielberg

Steven Spielberg (1947–   ), the director of many blockbuster films, was born in Cincinnati. His hits have included *E.T.: The Extraterrestrial, Raiders of the Lost Ark, Jurassic Park, Schindler's List,* and *Saving Private Ryan.*

Gloria Steinem (1934–), born in Toledo, is one of the country's leading activists for women's rights. She helped found *Ms.* magazine in 1972. Instead of focusing on makeup, clothing, hairstyles, or cooking, *Ms.* discusses political, social, and economic issues that are important to women. Steinem has continued to write and lecture on behalf of women's rights.

R. L. Stine (1943–) has made a career out of scaring the wits out of children. His *Goosebumps* book series, introduced in the early 1990s, has sold millions of copies. The stories even became a popular television series. Stine is a native of Bexley.

Carl B. Stokes (1927–1996) was born in Cleveland. When he was chosen to lead that city in 1967, he became the first African American elected mayor of a major American city. Later, Stokes served as the U.S. ambassador to the Seychelles, an island nation in the Indian Ocean.

William Howard Taft (1857–1930) was the twenty-seventh president of the United States. Born in Cincinnati, Taft served as a judge, territorial governor of the Philippines, and U.S. secretary of war before becoming president. After his presidency, Taft became chief justice of the U.S. Supreme Court, which made him the only ex-president to serve on the court.

Tecumseh (1768–1813), a Shawnee chief, was born near what is now the town of Xenia. One of the greatest Native-American leaders, Tecumseh hoped to unite all North American Indians against the whites, who had pushed the Shawnee further west. He was respected by both whites and

Indians for his courage and statesmanship. William Henry Harrison, governor of the Indiana Territory and later U.S. president, called him "one of those uncommon geniuses." He was killed in battle after siding with the British during the War of 1812.

James Thurber (1895–1961), humorist and author, was born in Columbus. Best known for his short story "The Secret Life of Walter Mitty," Thurber also wrote the books *My Life and Hard Times*, *The Thurber Carnival*, and *The Beast in Me and Other Animals*.

Lillian Wald (1867–1940) was born to an upper-middle-class Jewish family in Cincinnati but left her comfortable life to serve as a nurse in low-income neighborhoods in New York City. She organized the first visiting nurse service and school nurse program, both of which have spread around the world. She also worked for laws and programs to benefit the poor, especially children.

Orville (1871–1948) and **Wilbur Wright** (1867–1912) of Dayton made the world's first successful airplane flight. The brothers flew their motor-powered aircraft on December 17, 1903, at Kitty Hawk, North Carolina. The craft reached a speed of 7 to 9 miles per hour as it rose into the air. Each brother took a turn flying the plane for twelve seconds.

TOUR THE STATE

Toledo Museum of Art (Toledo) At this world-famous art collection, you can see everything from an Egyptian mummy and African sculpture to French furniture and American glassware.

Toledo Museum of Art

Kelleys Island (Kelleys Island) You can only reach this resort island in Lake Erie by boat, but it's worth the trip to see some of Ohio's ancient history. Inscription Rock is covered with picture drawings made by prehistoric Indians. The glacial grooves in Kelleys Island State Park were carved in solid stone by huge moving walls of ice more than 30,000 years ago.

Thomas Edison Birthplace Museum (Milan) The house where America's greatest inventor was born and lived as a boy looks much like it did in Edison's youth. Inside you can see replicas of Edison's greatest inventions.

The Rock and Roll Hall of Fame and Museum (Cleveland) The history of rock and roll is on display at this exciting lakefront museum. The guitars, clothes, and music of rock and roll's best are featured.

Cleveland Metroparks Zoo (Cleveland) More than three thousand creatures call this zoo home. Many animals, such as zebras, giraffes, ostriches, kangaroos, wallabies, and wolves, are found in realistic outdoor environments. The rain forest exhibit contains six hundred animals and 10,000 plants with a 25-foot waterfall and simulated thunderstorms.

Headlands Beach State Park (Mentor) Some of Lake Erie's best beaches are found in this park, which is great for swimming, playing, and picnicking. Nearby at the Mentor Marsh State Nature Preserve, there's also hiking and bird-watching.

Cuyahoga Valley National Recreation Area (Brecksville) Stretching along a 22-mile section of the Cuyahoga River, this park offers hiking, picnicking, biking, and canoeing. You can also explore old sections of the Ohio and Erie Canal where parts of the canal's locks and historic buildings still stand.

Burchfield Homestead Museum (Salem) At the childhood home of artist Charles Burchfield (1893–1967), visitors can step into rooms with outdoor views that inspired specific works of his art. Outside, the garden has been restored to look as it did in 1913 when Burchfield wrote about it in his journal.

Inventure Place (Akron) Learn about America's greatest inventors at this museum's National Inventors Hall of Fame, where the creators of everything from the cotton gin to the videotape recorder are highlighted. You can also experiment with strobe lights and electromagnets at hands-on exhibits.

Pro Football Hall of Fame (Canton) The legends of the game come alive in the city where pro football started in 1920. Bronze statues showcase the game's best players. Exhibits feature everything from old uniforms to Super Bowl rings. You can also watch football's greatest moments on video.

German Culture Museum (Walnut Creek) This museum is one of the best places to learn about Ohio's large Amish community. Exhibits about the Amish and other Swiss-German peoples who settled in the region include fine examples of their furniture, quilts, and folk art.

Schoenbrunn Village (New Philadelphia) This reconstructed mission village looks much like it did in 1771 when it was founded as a home for Christian Indians. Today, you can sit on the wood benches in the village's school and church and explore small cabins and a graveyard.

Campus Martius Museum (Marietta) The oldest cabin in Ohio is on display at this museum, along with other artifacts dealing with the early settlement of the Northwest Territory.

Hocking Hills State Park (Logan) Spectacular cliffs, caves, and waterfalls are found throughout this popular spot for hiking and picnicking. The Conkles Hollow area features multicolored sandstone cliffs over 200 feet high. Rock House is a cliffside cave with a number of "windows" looking out into a gorge.

Hocking Hills State Park

Ohio Historical Center and Ohio Village (Columbus) Trace Ohio's natural and human history with fun, hands-on exhibits at the historical center. You can test your knowledge with computer quizzes or touch a piece of petrified wood. Other displays include a giant mastodon skeleton and life-size replicas of Native-American dwellings. Ohio Village is a re-creation of a nineteeth-century Ohio town, complete with a school, blacksmith shop, doctor's office, and other buildings.

Hopewell Culture National Historical Park (Chillicothe) Twenty-three cone-shaped mounds built by the Hopewell Indians more than a thousand years ago can be found at this site in southern Ohio. Walking trails lead throughout the mounds, and the visitor center contains displays on the Hopewell culture.

Great Serpent Mound (Peebles) One of the best-preserved animal-shaped Indian mounds in the country, this curving snake is more than one-quarter of a mile long and about one thousand years old. You can walk around the entire mound or view it from an observation tower.

National Afro-American Museum and Cultural Center (Wilberforce) This museum focuses on the black experience in America. One exhibit features the history of African-American music, while another re-creates an African-American neighborhood from the 1950s.

National Museum of the United States Air Force (Dayton) The more than three hundred planes and missiles at this huge museum trace the history of the air force from its beginnings in the early 1900s to the present. You can see everything from the air force's very first planes to the massive B-36 bomber to the latest stealth fighter. You can also walk through the bomb bay of a nuclear bomber and sit in the cockpit of a modern jet fighter.

Dayton Aviation Heritage Historical Park (Dayton) The Wright Cycle Company Complex shows where the famous brothers Wilbur and Orville ran their printing business and then their bicycle shop. The Paul Laurence Dunbar State Memorial, located at this site, commemorates the life and work of this acclaimed African-American poet.

Cedar Bog Nature Preserve (Urbana) This unique bog is home to a number of rare and endangered plants and animals. From the boardwalk that twists through the preserve, you might glimpse a swamp rattlesnake, a spotted turtle, or an insect-eating sundew plant. The bog is also a good place for watching birds and butterflies.

Neil Armstrong Air & Space Museum (Wapakoneta) Dedicated to Ohio native Neil Armstrong, the first man on the moon, this museum traces the history of space travel. Displays include a jet fighter Armstrong flew as a test pilot and a Mercury space capsule. A sound tunnel and infinity room re-create what it feels like to be in space.

FUN FACTS

Ever wonder why the city of Cleveland's name isn't spelled like that of its founder, Moses Cleaveland? In 1830 the editor of a local newspaper, the *Cleveland Advertiser*, dropped the first "a" in "Cleaveland" so the title would fit on one line. The new spelling stuck.

Only in Zanesville would you get directions telling you to "go to the middle of the bridge and turn left." The city's famous Y-bridge is built at the intersection of the Muskingum and Licking Rivers. One span is built to the middle of the river, with spans forking to the left and right. It is believed to be the only Y-bridge in the world.

Annie Oakley, who was probably the best female sharpshooter ever, was born in Darke County. One day she hit 4,772 of 5,000 glass balls tossed in the air.

The first public library west of the Appalachian Mountains opened in Athens County in 1804. Called the Coonskin Library, it opened after two citizens took a wagonload of animal skins to Boston and returned with fifty-one books.

The little candy with the hole in the center, Life Savers, was invented in Cleveland in 1912. After his chocolate melted in the summer, candy-maker Clarence Crane made some hard mints, punched a hole in the middle of each, and sold them for five cents.

Find Out More

If you want to find out more about Ohio, check your local library or bookstore for these titles.

GENERAL STATE BOOKS

Deady, Kathleen W. *Ohio* (Portrait of the States). Milwaukee: Gareth Stevens, 2005.

Hart, Joyce. *Ohio* (It's My State!). Tarrytown, NY: Benchmark Books, 2006.

Kline, Nancy. *Ohio.* Danbury, CT: Children's Press, 2002.

Knapp, Ron. *Ohio.* Berkeley Heights, NJ: Enslow Publishers, 2002.

SPECIAL INTEREST BOOKS

Giblin, James Cross. *The Boy Who Saved Cleveland.* (historical fiction) New York: Henry Holt, 2006.

McNeese, Tim. *The Ohio River.* Broomall, PA: Chelsea House, 2004.

Schonberg, Marcia. *Ohio Native Peoples.* Chicago: Heinemann Library, 2003.

———. *Ohio Plants and Animals.* Chicago: Heinemann Library, 2003.

DVDS AND VIDEOS

Discoveries America—Ohio. Bennett-Watt Entertainment, 2004.

Ohio State—The History of Buckeye Football. Warner Home Video, 2005.

WEB SITES

Ohio Historical Society
www.ohiohistory.org/
Explore the history as well as the state historic sites and museums of Ohio.

Ohio & Erie Canalway
www.ohioanderiecanalway.com
This site explores the history of the Ohio and Erie Canal and provides visitor information and activities available at the park.

Rock and Roll Hall of Fame and Museum
www.rockhall.com/
Inductees, exhibits, general information about the museum, and programs at the museum can be found at this site.

Toledo Zoo
www.toledozoo.org
The Toledo Zoo's Web site offers visitors zoo happenings, an introduction to the animals and plants found at the zoo, and a kid's page.

Index

Page numbers in **boldface** are illustrations and charts.

ABOUT THE AUTHOR

Victoria Sherrow grew up in Salem, Ohio, a town with Quaker roots that was an important station on the Underground Railroad. She attended The Ohio State University.

She now has written more than sixty books for young people, including the one in this series about Connecticut, where she lives with her family.